Marilene Feitosa Soares

Tax Effects of the University for All Program (PROUNI)

Marilene Feitosa Soares

Tax Effects of the University for All Program (PROUNI)

Analysis of the Tax Effects of the University for All Program (PROUNI): Case Study

ScienciaScripts

Imprint
Any brand names and product names mentioned in this book are subject to trademark, brand or patent protection and are trademarks or registered trademarks of their respective holders. The use of brand names, product names, common names, trade names, product descriptions etc. even without a particular marking in this work is in no way to be construed to mean that such names may be regarded as unrestricted in respect of trademark and brand protection legislation and could thus be used by anyone.

Cover image: www.ingimage.com

This book is a translation from the original published under ISBN 978-620-2-40661-1.

Publisher:
Sciencia Scripts
is a trademark of
Dodo Books Indian Ocean Ltd. and OmniScriptum S.R.L publishing group

120 High Road, East Finchley, London, N2 9ED, United Kingdom
Str. Armeneasca 28/1, office 1, Chisinau MD-2012, Republic of Moldova, Europe
Managing Directors: Ieva Konstantinova, Victoria Ursu
info@omniscriptum.com

Printed at: see last page
ISBN: 978-620-0-75569-8

SUMMARY

To God,

for the fear of God is the beginning of wisdom.

ACKNOWLEDGEMENTS

To God, for all knowledge emanates from Him. To Him be eternal gratitude and thanks for always being the source of true science.

To my husband Paulo Roberto, for his tireless support.

To our daughters, Mariana and Isabella, for their understanding during the time I isolated myself for research.

To my mother and brothers, for the basic teachings of love and for their prayers, always.

To my dear teachers, for the knowledge they passed on to me.

To my colleagues on the Professional Master's Degree in Controllership, for the pleasant interaction during the course.

To everyone at VMF Consultores, for their encouragement and help in carrying out this work.

My special thanks go to Professor Terezinha de Jesus Pinheiro Maciel for her guidance, encouragement, suggestions, attention and dedication of her valuable time.

Thanks to Professor Sandra Maria dos Santos, who has contributed so much to my development, not only as coordinator of the master's course, but also as a teacher and co-supervisor, a woman dedicated to her work, an example to be followed.

To Professor Dr. Maria Isabel Filgueiras Lima Ciasca, for her willingness to sit on the examining board.

Finally, our thanks go to the many who have remained anonymous. However, there are those who also deserve to have their names recorded in this work as a token of our gratitude for their significant collaboration: Orlando Vieira, Kelma Marques, Edianez Bezerra, Ana Clàudia Madeiro Halliday, Janaina de Sousa Barbosa, Pr. Joao Venâncio, Nathàlia Benevides Monteiro, Cristina and Lùcio Grangeiro.

"PROUNI (University for All Program) was both the most creative and efficient way of socially including underprivileged students."

Ednilo Soàrez

ABSTRACT

The complexity of Brazilian tax legislation has increased the need for institutions to organize their businesses with a focus on tax planning in order to reduce their tax burden. Law No. 11,096 of January 13, 2005, which instituted the University for All Program (PROUNI), included the exemption of some federal taxes in exchange for full and partial scholarships granted by Higher Education Institutions to young low-income students. The objectives of this dissertation were to evaluate the tax effects observed in a private, for-profit higher education institution located in the municipality of Fortaleza, as a result of joining the University for All Program (PROUNI), to contextualize and describe the taxes related to the program and to relate the tax savings achieved to the investment supported by scholarships granted under PROUNI. The methodology was based on bibliographical and documentary research, using the single case study method. Various sources of evidence were used (interviews, accounting statements, financial reports, tax assessment spreadsheets and documents relating to the program). The results obtained show that the Private Higher Education Institution analyzed recovered all the taxes related to the University for All Program, failing to pay the Union's public coffers an average of 53% of the total taxes it owed, representing 4% of its turnover. It is important to note that the program has significantly increased the number of places in higher education, made free education more accessible in the country and contributed to combating social inequality.

Keywords: tax planning, PROUNI, Private Higher Education Institution, tax effects.

1 INTRODUCTION

The Brazilian tax burden (the sum of federal, state and municipal taxes collected), according to a study published by the Brazilian Institute of Tax Planning (IBPT), reached its highest level ever in 2006, 35.21% of the Gross Domestic Product - GDP (AMARAL; OLENIKE, 2006).

Brazil is among the countries that pay the most taxes in the world. Among the 24 countries evaluated in a survey carried out by the Brazilian Institute of Tax Planning (AMARAL; OLENIKE, 2006), Brazil's tax burden is second only to that of Sweden (50.7%), Norway (44.9%), France (43.7%) and Italy (42.2%). The weight of Brazilian taxes is the highest in Latin America and in developing countries.

The aforementioned authors state that 61 taxes are currently levied in the country, including duties, fees and contributions, as well as around 93 ancillary obligations that a company must fulfill in order to keep up with the tax authorities. In addition, Brazilian taxpayers will work from January 1st until May 25th, i.e. 145 days just to pay the taxes required by the federal, state and municipal governments.

International Business Communications has reported in studies that, on average, 33% (thirty-three percent) of turnover is used to pay taxes. Of the sum of costs and expenses, more than half is represented by taxes (IBC BRASIL, 2006).

A study called "The suppression of taxpayers' rights: 18 years of the 1988 Federal Constitution" (AMARAL; OLENIKE, 2006) reveals that the huge number of tax regulations is one of the causes of the increase in the tax burden. According to Gilberto Luiz do Amaral, president of IBPT, since the promulgation of the Federal Constitution almost 19 years ago, 3.5 million rules have been issued by the federal, state and municipal executives. Of this total, 229,616 refer to tax rules, which represents, on average, thirty-five tax rules per day.

The high tax burden in Brazil affects all business activities, and in the education sector, this reality is no different. According to tax expert Gandra (2006), the burden of educational taxes is one of the most significant in the country and has been one of the main obstacles to the development of educational institutions:

> the weight of taxes in the education sector needs to be reviewed and reduced by the government. Only in this way can education become a right for all and a duty of the state, as provided for in Article 205 of the Brazilian Constitution, because more than 40% of school fees are made up of taxes. This high tax burden contributes to increased default and stagnation in the sector. (GANDRA, 2006, p.3)

In recent years there has been rapid growth in the higher education sector, and in order to dribble the competition, private higher education institutions are seeking to benefit from effective strategies capable of improving their profitability and preserving their continuity in the market. One of the ways to achieve these goals is by planning the calculation and payment of their taxes, taking advantage of what tax legislation offers to reduce, eliminate or delay the tax burden.

The tool used to study the reduction of the tax burden within the dictates of tax legislation is tax planning, which according to Neves (2005, p.45), consists of the following

technique by which a person organizes their business with the aim of reducing or eliminating taxes. Tax planning takes the form of searching for hypotheses of non-incidence, exemptions and more favorable credits, always taking into account the business purpose.

Tax planning is not just a taxpayer's right, it is also an obligation that should be part of the business routine. Company directors have been given this task by corporate legislation, under the terms of articles 153 and 154 of Law 6.404 - the Companies Act (BRASIL, 1976). In this sense, Latorraca (1999, p. 63) also highlights the role of the administrator in the search for the best result from the point of view of tax savings:

the object of tax planning is ultimately tax savings. By weighing up the various legal options, the administrator obviously seeks to guide his steps in such a way as to avoid, whenever possible, the most onerous procedure from a tax point of view.

With the globalization of the economy, the correct management of the tax burden is a matter of business survival. Tax planning is legal and by carrying it out companies can capitalize their businesses, reduce their prices, invest, create jobs, and thus remain in the competitive market.

From the point of view of tax planning, private higher education institutions can choose to develop social projects that can be converted into tax rebates. The University for All Program (PROUNI) is a tax planning alternative that aims to minimize the tax burden on these entities.

PROUNI is a program created by the Federal Government through Provisional Measure No. 213 of 2004 and institutionalized by Law No. 11,096, which allows low-income young people access to higher education by granting full or partial scholarships offered by higher education institutions in Brazil in exchange for exemption from some federal taxes (BRASIL, 2005a).

Private higher education institutions (for profit or not) that join PROUNI will be exempt from the following taxes during the term of the agreement: Corporate Income Tax (IRPJ); Social Contribution on Net Profits (CSLL); Social Security Financing Contribution (COFINS), and Social Integration Program Contribution (PIS).

The panorama of higher education in Brazil has changed completely in the last five years, with an accelerated increase in the number of private institutions and a slight retraction in the number of public ones. Of the 1,859 higher education institutions in Brazil in 2003, according to the INEP/MEC census (2006), 1,652 were private and 207 public. Nevertheless, 37.5% (thirty-seven and a half percent) of the vacancies in private institutions, which corresponds to approximately half a million, are idle. In public education institutions, capacity is much better utilized, with only 5% (five percent) of vacancies unfilled.

In this context, the importance of the issue is not only due to the possibility of democratizing access to higher education for the underprivileged population from the public system and raising educational standards, but also, from a business point of view, due to the possibility of reducing the tax burden currently faced by private higher education institutions in Brazil.

From an academic point of view, this study can be justified by its exploratory nature, since PROUNI was instituted recently and little research has been carried out, especially in the tax field, and can therefore serve as a basis for other research that could be carried out.

The high tax burden currently experienced by private higher education institutions means that they are looking to tax planning for strategies to reduce the high tax burden. Law No. 11.096 (BRASIL, 2005a) allows private institutions that join PROUNI to be exempt from IRPJ, CSLL, PIS and COFINS. Exemption from IRPJ and CSLL is conditional on the existence of profits, so there may or may not be tax savings on certain courses. As for PIS and COFINS, since they are levied on turnover, they generate certain tax savings. It also remains to be seen whether the overall savings per course outweigh the investment in scholarships made available by the institution that joined the program.

In view of this, the question arises: what tax effects can be observed in a private, for-profit higher education institution located in the municipality of Fortaleza, as a result of joining the University for All Program (PROUNI)?

According to Trivinos (1987, p.105), by establishing hypotheses or assumptions, the researcher envisages probable solutions. A hypothesis involves a possible truth, a probable outcome. It is a pre-established truth, intuited, with the support of theory or practice. In the light of this concept, the assumptions established to guide this study are as follows:

a) PROUNI is a useful tool for tax planning that can contribute to reducing the tax burden of private higher education institutions;

b) a private higher education institution that has joined PROUNI will achieve savings on PIS and COFINS, as the basis for calculating these taxes is turnover;

c) if the institution makes a profit, there will be tax savings on IRPJ and CSLL, since these taxes are levied on profit;

d) even if it has an overall tax loss (based on the consolidated result), or a low operating profit, the institution may have a specific tax profit on some degree courses, and as a result, and for management purposes, it will be able to identify the courses that generate the greatest tax savings as a result of joining PROUNI;

e) The degree course with the highest number of paying students must also be the one that contributed most to the increase in tax savings, and

f) the tax savings achieved by the institution must be at least equal to the investment in scholarships, corresponding to the value of the tuition fees not received as a result of joining PROUNI.

According to Richardson (1980, p.62), "the objectives should be drawn directly from the problems. They can even be divided into general and specific". The general objective refers to what is intended to be achieved by carrying out the research, while the specific objectives represent the stages to be completed in the process of achieving the general objective.

Thus, the main objective of this research was to evaluate the tax effects achieved by a private, for-profit Higher Education Institution located in the municipality of Fortaleza as a result of joining the University for All Program (PROUNI).

In order to achieve the general objective, the following specific objectives were drawn up:

a) contextualize the University for All Program (PROUNI);

b) describe the taxes related to PROUNI, and

c) relate the tax savings achieved to the investment made by the

institution with scholarships granted under PROUNI.

This dissertation is structured in seven chapters. In the introductory chapter (1), the proposed topic is contextualized, the relevance of the research is justified, the problem to be investigated is formulated, the general and specific objectives to be achieved are set out, ending with the presentation of the structure of the work.

The second chapter contains part of the theoretical framework, highlighting tax planning as a tool for reducing the tax burden. Initially, Brazil's current tax burden was analyzed according to surveys by the Brazilian Institute of Tax Planning (IBPT). Next, the concepts and purposes of taxes and tax planning were presented; the difference between tax planning and crimes against the tax order and, finally, the relationship between tax planning and the University for All Program (PROUNI).

The third chapter contextualized the University for All Program (PROUNI), presenting its concept, adhesion, disengagement, obligations, exemption and penalties, in accordance with specific legislation.

The fourth chapter takes a general approach to the taxes related to the University for All Program (PROUNI), namely: Corporate Income Tax (IRPJ), Social Contribution on Net Profits (CSL), Social Contribution for the Financing of Social Security (COFINS) and Contribution to the Social Integration Program (PIS).

The methodology was discussed in the fifth chapter and followed the guidance of Trivinos (1987, p. 109), who says that at this stage "the researcher defines the research plan", and Gil (2002), who describes the case study in stages. The methodological procedures describe the characterization of the research, the design, data collection, the objective of the study and the analysis and interpretation of the data. The methodology described in this chapter is defined as bibliographical and documentary research, using the single case study method carried out in a private higher education institution located in the city of Fortaleza.

In the sixth chapter, the results obtained in the study were presented and analyzed. The taxes covered by PROUNI (IRPJ, CSLL, PIS and COFINS) owed by Private Higher Education Institutions were calculated, based on the consolidated results and revenues for each degree course, from January 2005 to June 2006. Also in this chapter, the investments in scholarships made by the institutions surveyed were analyzed and compared with the tax savings generated as a result of joining PROUNI.

Finally, the conclusions of the study are presented, which seek to answer the research problem and suggest recommendations for future research on the subject. References and annexes are also presented.

2 TAX PLANNING

Before conceptualizing and defining the purposes of tax planning and commenting on crimes against the tax order, we discuss the Brazilian tax burden, its evolution, the factors that have contributed to its excessive increase, the comparison with the tax burden of 23 other countries and the time Brazilians have to work to pay taxes in Brazil.

2.1 Brazilian tax burden

The tax burden is a subject that arouses the interest of the whole of Brazilian society, both because it significantly burdens production and wages, and because of the complexity of the tax system.

The specialized literature is not concerned with defining the tax burden. The bodies and organizations that measure it try to define it according to the methodology they use to calculate it.

According to the Federal Court of Auditors (TCU), a country's tax burden represents the share of resources that the state compulsorily withdraws from individuals and companies, as the main way of financing all government activities. The economic concept of tax burden is the ratio between total tax revenue and the country's Gross Domestic Product (GDP) in a given fiscal year.

2.1.1 Methodology of the Brazilian Tax Burden Study

The Brazilian Institute of Tax Planning (IBPT) regularly monitors the tax burden. In the public sector, the Secretariat for Tax Affairs of the National Economic Development Bank (BNDES), the Brazilian Institute of Geography and Statistics (IBGE), the Federal Court of Auditors (TCU) and the Federal Revenue Secretariat (SRF) carry out the same survey. There is, therefore, no official calculation methodology, which means that each of the entities or bodies uses different criteria, leading to divergences between the results, without, however, compromising the objectives of each of them, which is to provide information on the amount of resources transferred from the economy to the federal, state and municipal governments (AMARAL; OLENIKE, 2006).

The surveys carried out by the aforementioned bodies use the same database for calculating revenue, i.e. they take into account taxes administered by the Federal Revenue Office, INSS and Caixa Econômica Federal, CONFAZ - National Council for Finance Policy. However, the differences between the methodologies of the studies lie in a few factors, as IBPT (AMARAL; OLENIKE, 2006) reports:

a) Federal Revenue Service: does not take into account the amounts collected as fines, interest and monetary correction ; estimates municipal tax collections; does not take into account collections as union contributions, to professional practice inspection bodies;

b) IBGE: does not take into account improvement fees and contributions that are offset by the provision of services, and completely disregards the amounts relating to the social security contributions of federal civil servants and military personnel;

c) BNDES: does not make an estimate of municipal taxes, through a preliminary survey of the collections of the three main capitals (Sao Paulo, Rio de Janeiro and Belo Horizonte); and makes an estimate of the values of other taxes whose collection is not known, using the same variation as the known taxes;

d) TCU: The methodology used by the TCU considers in the calculation of the tax burden, the tax revenue itself, according to art. 5 of the CTN (BRAZIL, 1966), i.e. taxes, fees and improvement contributions;

e) IBPT: considers all the amounts collected by the three spheres of government (taxes plus fines, interest and correction), including revenues from union contributions, to professional practice inspection bodies and court fees; for the survey of state and Federal District collections it uses as a database, in addition to CONFAZ, the figures released by the State Finance Secretariats and the National Treasury Secretariat of the Ministry of Finance, as some states are slow to submit their reports to CONFAZ; with regard to municipal revenue, it monitors the figures published by the 845 municipalities that publish their figures in compliance with the Fiscal Responsibility Law, and also through the figures published by the National Treasury Secretariat and the State Audit Courts.

The surveys carried out by the IBPT were selected as the basis for this study, as their calculations take into account more complex data in relation to the taxes collected in Brazil.

2.1.2 The Evolution of the Tax Burden

According to a study published by the Brazilian Institute of Tax Planning - IBPT, the Brazilian tax burden in relation to GDP - Gross Domestic Product in 2006 reached 35.21% (thirty-five integers and twenty-one hundredths percent), compared to 34.12% (thirty-four integers and twelve hundredths percent) in 2005, which represents an increase of 1.09 percentage points (AMARAL; OLENIKE, 2005).

The collection of all federal, state and municipal taxes totaled R$392.78 billion in the first half of 2006 alone, of which 69% (sixty-nine percent) were federal taxes, 26% (twenty-six percent) state taxes and 5% (five percent) municipal taxes. Furthermore, compared to the first half of 2005, there was an increase in collection of 8.97% (eight integers and ninety-seven hundredths percent).

Table 1 shows the evolution of the Brazilian tax burden in relation to GDP, from 1986 to 2006.

TABLE 1 - General tax collection: In US$ million (1986 to 1991)/R$ million (1992 onwards)

Year	GDP	Taxes			Total tax collection	% of GDP	Tax burden growth compared
		Federal	State	Municipal			

							to the previous year (%)
1986	337.832	56.386	17.160	2.095	75.641	22,39%	
1987	360.810	55.048	16.015	2.093	73.156	20,28%	-2,11
1988	371.999	55.542	16.656	2.232	74.430	20,01%	-0,27
1989	399.647	58.544	27.613	2.398	88.555	22,16%	2,15
1990	398.747	79.352	36.219	3.684	119.255	29,91%	7,75
1991	405.679	65.386	29.686	4.781	99.853	24,61%	-5,33
1992	355.453	60.437	26.297	3.480	90.214	25,38%	0,77
1993	429.968	79.510	25.398	2.971	107.879	25,09%	-0,29
1994	477.920	98.199	34.334	4.200	136.733	28,61%	3,52
1995	646.192	124.695	53.139	9.024	186.858	28,92%	0,31
1996	843.966	139.484	62.980	10.116	212.581	25,19%	-3,73
1997	939.147	158.566	69.320	11.305	239.191	25,47%	0,28
1998	979.276	181.828	72.070	14.219	268.117	27,38%	1,91
1999	1.065.000	210.691	79.154	15.096	304.941	28,63%	1,25
2000	1.179.482	250.302	95.383	16.011	361.696	30,67%	2,03
2001	1.302.136	278.599	108.262	16.884	403.745	31,01%	0,34
2002	1477.822	341.007	122.234	18.742	482.361	32,65%	1,64
2003	1.669.948	391.052	139.137	22.990	553.179	32,54%	-0,110
2004	1.941.498	454.313	166.117	29.705	650.135	33,49%	0,95
2005	2.147.944	514.417	187.873	30.574	732.864	34,12%	0,63
2006	2.322.818	570.789	211.956	35.193	817.938	35,21%	1,09

Source: Amaral and Olenike (2006).

Table 1 shows that from 1986 to 2006, the tax burden increased by 12.82 percentage points, and this increase was quite significant from 1999 onwards (6.58%). In the first year of President Luis Inâcio Lula da Silva's government, the tax burden rose by 2.56 percentage points.

2.1.3 Current Tax Reality

As can be seen in section 2.1.2, in recent years the discussion about the exorbitant evolution of the tax burden has intensified in the country, especially its accelerated rise since the 1990s. Experts point to certain factors that have contributed to the tax burden reaching its current level.

According to the IBPT (AMARAL; OLENIKE, 2006), the following factors cause taxpayers to feel uncertain about whether or not they are complying with all the obligations demanded by the tax authorities:

a) firstly, because of the approximately 61 (sixty-one) taxes levied in Brazil, including taxes, fees and contributions;

b) secondly, because of the number of rules governing the tax system. There are more than 200,000 tax rules which represent, on average, 35 (thirty-five) tax rules per day. Therefore, taxpayers must be aware of this number of rules in order to be up to date with the tax authorities;

c) thirdly, because of the 93 (ninety-three) ancillary obligations that a company must fulfill in order to keep up with the tax authorities: declarations, forms, books, forms, etc. The cost to companies of complying with accessory obligations is around 1% (one percent) of their turnover, and

d) lastly, because of the cumulative nature of taxes: multiple incidences on the same calculation basis and several times in the production chain, known as the cascade effect: CPMF levied on PIS/COFINS, levied on ICMS, levied on INSS, and so on.

In 2004, the IBPT carried out a study of the Brazilian tax burden compared to 23 other countries that make up the world's largest economies.

TABLE 2 - World tax burden in relation to GDP (%) - 2004

Country	2004 (%)
Sweden	50,7
Norway	44,9
France	43,7
Italy	42,2
Brazil (IBPT)	36,8
Brazil (Receita Federal)	35,91
United Kingdom	36,1
Germany	34,6
Turkey	31,1
Canada	33,0
Spain	35,1
New Zealand	35,4
Switzerland	29,4
Portugal	36,4
Poland	34,2
Australia	31,6
United States	25,4
Ireland	25,3
Japan	25,3
South Korea	24,6
Argentina	21,9
Chile	19,2
Mexico	18,5
China	16,7
Russia	16,9

Source: Amaral and Olenike (2005).

From the IBPT study shown in table 2, it can be seen that Brazil has a higher tax burden than 21 other countries, behind only France and Italy, considering that Sweden and Norway don't have bigger economies than Brazil.

Brazilian taxpayers still have to work four months and 25 days of the year just to pay the taxes demanded by the government, in other words, they are working from January 1st until May 25th of each year. This is shown in Table 3, a study carried out by the IBPT in the years 1986 to 2006.

TABLE 3 - Average days worked per year to pay taxes in Brazil - (1986 to 2006)

Year	Days	Months
1986	82	2 months and 22 days
1987	74	2 months and 14 days
1988	73	2 months and 13 days
1989	81	2 months and 21 days
1990	109	3 months and 19 days
1991	90	3 months
1992	93	3 months and 3 days
1993	92	3 months and 2 days
1994	104	3 months and 14 days

1995	106	3 months and 16 days
1996	100	3 months and 10 days
1997	100	3 months and 10 days
1998	107	3 months and 17 days
1999	115	3 months and 25 days
2000	121	4 months and 1 day
2001	130	4 months and 10 days
2002	133	4 months and 13 days
2003	135	4 months and 15 days
2004	138	4 months and 18 days
2005	140	4 months and 20 days
2006	145	4 months and 25 days

Source: Amaral; Olenike (2006).

In the survey carried out by IBPT, as shown in Table 3, taxes levied on income (salaries, fees, etc.) are taken into account, which is mainly made up of Personal Income Tax (IRPF), INSS contributions and social security contributions. In addition, there are taxes on consumption, which are already built into the price of the products and services purchased (PIS, COFINS, ICMS, IPI, ISS, etc.), as well as taxes on property (IPTU, IPVA, ITCMD, ITBI, ITR). It's worth noting that taxpayers also pay other taxes, such as fees (public cleaning, garbage collection, issuing documents and contributions, public lighting, etc.).

In addition, based on studies carried out by the IBPT, the days worked in Brazil to pay taxes were compared with the days worked by taxpayers in other countries. In Mexico, it takes 91 working days to pay taxes, while in Brazil it takes 145 days, as shown in Table 1.

Country	Days worked
Sweden	185 days
France	149 days
Brazil	145 days
Spain	137 days
United States	102 days
Argentina	97 days
Chile	92 days
Mexico	91 days

TABLE 1 - Comparison of days worked to pay taxes in Brazil with other countries

Source: Amaral; Olenike (2006).

Finally, based on IBPT surveys, it was found that the average corporate tax burden consumes 33.05% (thirty-three and five-tenths percent) of turnover, 47.14% (forty-seven and fourteen-hundredths percent) of costs and expenses and 52.23% (fifty-two and twenty-three-hundredths percent) of a company's profits.

Faced with the reality to which they are exposed, taxpayers can and should seek legal and lawful alternatives to reduce their tax burden. Currently, the most widely used methodology for obtaining a lower tax burden is the so-called Tax Planning.

2.2 The concept of tax planning

Nowadays, the debate around what is commonly called "tax planning" is settled in legislation and doctrine, as well as being accepted by the tax authorities themselves, that taxpayers have the right to organize their businesses and their assets in the least onerous way possible.

Based on the idea that taxpayers are free to organize their lives in such a way as to pay the lowest tax burden, various tax experts have commented on tax planning.

Greco (2004, p. 109) conceptualizes "tax planning" as a constitutional right:

> this search for the lowest tax burden legally possible involves the use of an individual freedom honored by the Constitution; whether in the freedom of initiative (CF/88, article 1, IV and article 170, *caput*), or in free competition (article 170, IV), or in the pure freedoms of article 5, there is the freedom of each person to organize their life which is expressed, predominantly, in the exercise of contractual freedom. In short, the constitutional order enshrines a freedom for the citizen and so-called tax planning arises from the idea of exercising a freedom to set up one's own business, to organize one's life in such a way as to pay as little tax as legally possible.

Within this constitutional precept, it is clear that taxpayers can (have freedom) and must structure their businesses in the best possible way (self-organization), always seeking to reduce their costs, including taxes, always paying attention to legality.

Tax planning is not just a taxpayer's right, it is also an obligation that must be part of the business routine. Company directors have been given this task by corporate legislation, under the terms of articles 153 and 154 of Law No. 6.404 - the Companies Act: (BRASIL, 1976)

> Article 153. In carrying out his duties, the director of the company must use the care and diligence that every active and upright man usually uses in managing his own affairs.
>
> Art. 154. Directors must exercise the powers conferred on them by law and the articles of association in order to achieve the purposes and in the interests of the company, while meeting the requirements of the public good and the company's social function. (emphasis added)

The articles mentioned above confer on company directors the care and zeal that they must maintain for the smooth running of the business, and tax planning is a tool that can support them in this mission.

Rocha (*apud* Rolim, 1998, p. 52-53) writes about tax planning:

> tax planning, when carried out in a lawful manner, is a branch of tax administration and should also be considered as a business routine activity of significant importance, especially when the Legislator itself has imposed on the administrator the duty to employ the resources - obviously, legal ones - that are within his reach, in order to achieve the ends and in the interests of the company.

Tax planning must be applied lawfully and, as it is a management support tool that contributes to the success and growth of companies, it must be incorporated into their activities on an ongoing basis.

Latorraca (2000, p. 63) also highlights the role of the administrator in the search for the best result from the point of view of tax savings:

> The object of tax planning is ultimately tax savings. By weighing up the various legal options, the administrator obviously seeks to guide his steps in such a way as to avoid, whenever possible, the least onerous procedure from a tax point of view.

It follows, therefore, that among the various alternatives offered by tax legislation, the taxpayer will be able to plan in such a way as to choose the one that will bring him the least tax burden. Machado (2000, p. 51) describes:

> The doctrine has held that taxpayers have the right to arrange their business, their fortune, their way of life, in such a way as to pay the least tax or to pay no tax at all, as long as they do not violate any legal rules.

Thus, in Brazil, there has been an "explosion" of tax planning as a habitual practice of companies. Taxpayers have every right to organize their businesses and thus incur tax savings, without failing to comply with tax requirements.

With the globalization of the economy, the correct management of the tax burden is a matter of business survival, as it represents one of the largest portions of companies' costs. Tax planning is legal and healthy for the taxpayer's pocket. With it, companies can capitalize their businesses, reduce their prices, invest, create jobs and remain competitive in the market.

2.3 Purposes of tax planning

The main purpose of tax planning is to legally reduce the amount of tax due. In this context, Tôrres (2001, p. 37-38) describes:

> With the expression "tax planning" one must designate only the technique of preventive organization of business, aiming at a legitimate saving of taxes, regardless of any reference to the acts subsequently carried out.
>
> The lawful attitudes that may be adopted by taxpayers when structuring or reorganizing their businesses, with the aim of saving taxes, either by avoiding their incidence or by reducing or deferring the respective tax impact on operations, corresponds to the notion of "legitimate tax saving". Of course, there can be tax planning with an illicit content, but in this case, even if the object is illicit, the act of planning will always be lawful, so it is not rigorous to attribute an illicit act to the conduct of organizing business, preventively.
>
> [...] tax planning is nothing more than a preventive "test" technique that the operator carries out of the legal system, assessing future events in the light of the legal system in force, in a projection of the legal system onto subsequent events. It is a technique of subsumption in advance, foreseeing the legal and tax consequences, designed to act in accordance with the legal system, using the least onerous operations available as legitimate. For this reason, its content must take into account all the repercussions of the system, not only the strict tax rule, the one that defines the main tax obligation; but also all possible obligations: accessory (instrumental or formal duties), criminal etc. (emphasis added).

According to Amaral (2006), the exercise of tax planning seeks to achieve three objectives, namely

a) avoiding the incidence of tax

In this case, preventive studies are carried out on a legal basis, i.e. measures are taken to avoid the taxable event occurring. Once the taxable event has occurred, the tax obligation arises and the will of the parties is irrelevant to changing it.

The taxpayer can anticipate the taxable event with the aim of planning and sizing it up in such a way as to allow him to adopt, among the legal options available, those that are most convenient for him. Hence the fundamental importance of identifying when the taxable event occurs.

Any measure aimed at saving taxes will only be legitimate if it is taken before the taxable event occurs, always strictly observing the legal precepts. In short, the taxable event is the taxpayer's point of reference.

b) reducing the amount of tax

Preventive action in this case consists of seeking, where possible, legal means to reduce the rate or basis of calculation of the tax.

c) delay payment of the tax

In this case, taxpayers should adopt measures to postpone (delay) the payment of the tax, thus avoiding the payment of tax penalties (fines).

2.4 Crimes against the tax order

Taxpayers who intend to use tax planning should be very clear that planning does not consist of failing to pay what is due and not questionable, and should be careful not to run the risk of committing crimes against the tax order, and instead of reducing the tax burden for companies, causing great losses.

Law No. 8.137 (BRASIL, 1990) establishes criminal offenses against the tax order, which lists a series of crimes with prison sentences ranging from six months to five years, the text of which is as follows:

Art. 1 - It is a crime against the tax order to suppress or reduce taxes, or social contributions and any accessory, by means of the following conducts:

I - omitting information or making a false statement to the tax authorities;

II - defrauding the tax authorities by inserting inaccurate information or omitting transactions of any kind in documents or books required by tax law;

III - falsifying or altering invoices, invoices, duplicates, bills of sale or any other document relating to a taxable transaction;

IV - preparing, distributing, supplying, issuing or using a document which he knows or should know to be false or inaccurate;

V - denying or failing to provide, when obligatory, an invoice or equivalent document relating to the sale of goods or the provision of services actually carried out, or providing it in disagreement with the legislation.

Art. 2 - The following are crimes of the same nature

I - making a false declaration or omitting to declare income, assets or facts, or employing other fraud, in order to exempt oneself, in whole or in part, from paying a tax;

II - failing to pay, within the legal time limit, the amount of a tax or social contribution, deducted or collected, as the subject of an obligation and which he should have paid into the public coffers;

III - demand, pay or receive, for himself or for the beneficiary taxpayer, a percentage of the deductible or deducted portion of the tax or contribution as a tax incentive;

IV - failing to apply, or applying in breach of the regulations, tax incentives or tax installments released by development agencies or entities;

V - use or disclose a data processing program that allows the person liable to pay the tax to have accounting information other than that which is, by law, provided to the Public Treasury.

From the above, it can be seen that trying to circumvent the law in order to misappropriate the amount of tax owed to the State, constitutes a crime against the tax order.

2.4.1 Tax evasion, fraud, collusion and simulation

The act of planning to reduce taxes relating to past events , i.e. those that have already occurred, constitutes tax evasion, fraud and simulation. Latorraca (1985, p.20) argues that "there is only evasion when someone tries to simulate, hide or mischaracterize (evade) the taxable event (which has already occurred); or even simulate or conceal personal conditions that could affect the tax obligation".

Under the terms of Article 71 of Law No. 4.502 (BRASIL, 1964), tax evasion is understood to be any intentional action or omission aimed at preventing or delaying, in whole or in part, the knowledge of the tax authority:

a) the occurrence of the event giving rise to the main tax obligation, its nature or material circumstances;

b) the taxpayer's personal circumstances, which may affect the main tax obligation or corresponding tax credit.

Tax evasion is, therefore, the act in which the taxpayer has underpaid or failed to pay the tax due and collected by law, in other words, it is the misappropriation of the amount of tax that should have been passed on to the state.

Article 72 of Law No. 4.502 (BRASIL, 1964) states that 'fraud is any intentional action or omission aimed at preventing or delaying, in whole or in part, the occurrence of the taxable event or at excluding or modifying its essential characteristics, so as to reduce the amount of tax due'.

Campos (1985, p.19) writes that:

It is fundamental that the action or omission of tax planning is practiced and formalized before the occurrence of the taxable event, because any action or omission practiced and formalized after the occurrence of the taxable event, which aims to prevent or delay the occurrence of the taxable event, or reduce its economic effects, is considered fraud, as it implies tax evasion.

It is important to establish the basic difference between tax planning and

fraud. If the facts that actually occurred are proven through the tax books and documents, this is tax planning, but if what appears in the tax books and documents is different from the facts, this is fraud.

Fraud is therefore malicious deception or cunning action taken in bad faith to conceal the truth or evade compliance with a duty.

Collusion is the malicious agreement between two or more persons, natural or legal

aimed at the effects of tax evasion or fraud (Law No. 4.502/1964, Art. 73), thus representing the malicious combination of two people with the intention of deceiving a third person.

The concept of simulation is contained in Law 10.604 (BRASIL, 2002), the current civil code, in the sense that there will be simulation in legal acts in general, when:

a) they confer or transmit rights to persons other than those to whom they are actually conferred or transmitted;

b) they contain an untrue declaration, confession, condition or clause;

c) the private instruments are antedated or postdated.

In the act of simulation, there is the taxpayer's intention to simulate a misleading situation before the tax authorities.

Article 150 of the National Tax Code (BRASIL, 1966) adds that if simulation is established, the tax authorities may demand the tax at any time.

2.5 Tax planning in private higher education institutions

The high cost of taxes in Brazil affects all business activities, and in the education sector, this reality is no different. In the assessment of tax expert Gandra (2006), the weight of educational taxes is one of the highest in the country and has been one of the main obstacles to the development of educational institutions:

> the weight of taxes in the education sector needs to be reviewed and reduced by the government. Only in this way can education become a right for all and a duty of the state, as provided for in article 205 of the Brazilian Constitution, because more than 40% of school fees are made up of taxes. This high tax burden contributes to increased default and stagnation in the sector.

The federal government must emphasize Brazilian education, and for this reason, it must encourage private institutions to participate in this process, and one of the ways to count on this partnership is to exempt them from the exorbitant tax burden.

In the same vein, says the vice-president of the São Paulo Private Schools Union - SIEESP (2006):

what we need and demand is a fairer policy that is appropriate to the services we receive. On the other hand, by reducing this burden, we could give schools greater conditions to invest in technology, development and planning to further improve the quality of teaching. And thus make room for more students in private schools.

By not paying certain taxes, there will be money left over for the institutions to invest in the quality of teaching and the structure of schools. For this very reason, the government should refrain from collecting some taxes from private higher education institutions.

Table 2 shows the tax burden currently faced by private higher education institutions.

Tax base	**Tax base**	**Rates**
Billing	PIS	0,65%
	COFINS	3%
	IRPJ	4,80%
	CSLL	2,80%
	ISS	2% a 5%
Payroll	INSS - Company	20%
	INSS on Third Parties	4,50%
	Workman's Compensation Insurance	1%
	FGTS	8%
	FGTS Social Contribution	0,50%
Share Capital	Employer's Union Contribution	0,02% a 0,8%
Financial Transactions	CPMF	0,38%
	IOF	1,50%

TABLE 2 - Main taxes owed by for-profit private higher education institutions

Source: Prepared by the author based on tax legislation.

Table 2 does not include fees, improvement contributions and indirect taxes such as IPTU and IPVA.

By analyzing the tax burden shown in Table 2, it can be seen that there are many taxes owed by Private Higher Education Institutions for Profit, which is why they must consider managing their tax obligations as a daily necessity. This management of obligations is called tax planning, as mentioned above, and therefore consists of a lawful attitude aimed at reducing tax obligations.

Competitiveness in the education sector increasingly requires dynamic and innovative strategies capable of improving results (profitability). It is in this respect that tax planning should be seen by the managers of educational institutions as an indispensable tool for reducing their taxes and an essential weapon for their survival.

Through tax planning, the researched institution was suggested to join PROUNI as a tool capable of reducing its tax burden.

2.6 Taxes: Concept and Species

In order to provide a better understanding of the subject, the concept and species of taxes are described below, as well as the concept of tax exemption.

The definition of a tax is set out in Article 3 of the National Tax Code - CTN (BRASIL, 1966):

Art. 3: A tax is any compulsory pecuniary payment, in currency or the value of which can be expressed therein, which does not constitute a penalty for an unlawful act, established by law and levied by means of a fully binding administrative activity.

For a better understanding of the definition of a tax, it is possible to break it down into the following characteristics

definition into the following characteristics:

a) pecuniary payment: the legal concept excludes any payment that is not represented by money. Therefore, taxes cannot be paid with goods, labor or services;

b) compulsory: refers to the obligation to pay the tax regardless of the taxpayer's will;

c) in currency or whose value can be expressed in it: taxes can be set in currency (real), or in another unit translatable into currency, for example, indexers (ORTN, OTN, BTN, UFIR);

d) which does not constitute the sanction of an illegal act: the payment of a tax does not result from an infraction, so penalties (fines) are not included in the concept of a tax;

e) established by law: taxes can only be demanded by law (principle of legality: "no one shall be obliged to do or refrain from doing anything except by virtue of the law" - Art. 150, I, of the Federal Constitution (BRASIL, 1988a);

f) levied through a fully binding administrative activity: being administrative, this is a private activity that cannot be carried out by anyone else. Furthermore, it must be binding - not discretionary - meaning that the public administration must act strictly in accordance with the tax law, and not at its own discretion. Thus, the tax authorities have the power and the duty to collect.

Thus, a tax is defined as a certain amount of money that taxpayers (individuals and legal entities) are obliged to pay to the State (Union, States, Federal District and Municipalities) when they carry out certain triggering events provided for in tax laws.

As far as the types of taxes are concerned, the National Tax System is structured in such a way as to allow the State to collect:

a) taxes: the definition of a tax is in art. 16 of the CTN (BRASIL, 1966). What makes a tax special is that it is levied without the need for the state to provide something to the taxpayer in a timely manner, and that it will be levied according to the taxpayer's economic capacity, as set out in Art. 145, I, § 1 of the Federal Constitution (BRASIL, 1988a);

b) fees: fees are laid down in Article 145, II of the Federal Constitution (BRASIL, 1988) and Article 77 of the CTN and are linked to the actual use by the taxpayer of specific public services;

c) improvement contributions: these were created to cover the cost of public works resulting in real estate appreciation for the taxpayer, as set out in article 149 of the Federal Constitution (BRASIL, 1988a).

With the enactment of the 1988 Federal Constitution, social contributions were introduced to finance social activities, based on company profits, employee payroll and company turnover. They are currently divided into contributions to the INSS, the Trade Union Contribution, the PIS/Pasep Contribution, the Social Contribution on Net Profits and the Contribution to the Social Investment Fund (COFINS).

2.6.1 Tax exemption

Exemption is considered to be a tax favor (tax waiver by the state) where payment of the tax is excluded by law.

In the words of Cassone (1992, p.85) exemption is the legal dispensation from paying a certain tax, which is usually granted in the light of relevant regional, sectoral or national social and economic interest.

In the specific case of private institutions, this tax exemption is justified because it deals directly with education, which is everyone's right.

According to Sousa (1975, p. 97), "exemption is a tax favor granted by law, which consists of dispensing with the payment of a tax due".

This concept is identified in the National Tax Code (CTN) in articles 175 and 176, transcribed below (BRASIL, 1966):

Art. 175. The following are excluded from the tax credit:

I - Exemption;

II - amnesty

[...]

Art. 176. Exemption, even when provided for in a contract, shall always be the result of a law specifying the conditions and requirements for its concession, the taxes to which it applies and, if applicable, the period of duration.

Sole Paragraph. The exemption may be restricted to a certain region of the taxing entity's territory, due to conditions peculiar to it.

Tax exemptions can be granted for a certain or indefinite period, by means of an ordinary law, a complementary law, a legislative decree of the National Congress, or a state or district legislative decree.

Taxpayers favored by a specific exemption, or any other type of tax incentive, for a certain period of time, have an acquired right to enjoy it until the end of the term provided for in the law. In the case of PROUNI, the exemption was granted for a fixed period of time and was granted by ordinary law.

Exemption, as a rule, refers only to taxes. However, it does not prevent exemptions from being granted in relation to other types of tax (fees and contributions), provided that the law expressly states this (art. 177 of the CTN). This is what happens in the case of PROUNI, Law 11.096 (BRASIL, 2005a), which provides for an exemption from Corporate Income Tax (IRPJ), Social Contribution on Net Profits (CSLL), Social Integration Program (PIS) and Social Security Financing Contribution (COFINS).

This chapter covers: the evolution of the tax burden in Brazil, the concept and purposes of tax planning, crimes against the tax order and tax planning in Higher Education Institutions Private. The operating rules of the University for All Program (PROUNI) are described in the following chapter.

3 UNIVERSITY FOR ALL PROGRAM (PROUNI)

Various studies have highlighted the current low level of education among the Brazilian population. The low rate of students entering university is worrying. According to surveys carried out by the Ministry of Education, only nine percent (9%) of Brazilians between the ages of 18 and 24 currently obtain a place in higher education.

From 1999 to 2000, UNESCO carried out comparative studies of Brazil with other countries on the rate of schooling in higher education. According to IBGE (2006), this rate is calculated by considering the "proportion of people in a given age group who attend school in relation to the total population in the same age group". The study resulted in the data shown in Table 4.

TABLE 4 - Gross enrolment rate in higher education in selected countries - 1999/2000

Country	Gross enrollment rate
South Korea	72
USA	72
Argentina	48
Portugal	47
Chile	38
Uruguay	34
Bolivia	33
Colombia	22
Cuba	21
Mexico	20
Brazil	15
South Africa	15
Paraguay	14

Source: Adapted from UNESCO, *Global Education Digest* (2003) cited by Pinto (2004, p. 3).

The data presented shows that Brazil is in an extremely unfavorable position compared to other countries. The number of places occupied by Brazilian universities is only close to that offered by Paraguay and South Africa. Compared to the United States, Brazil is at a huge disadvantage. This leads to the conclusion that the country is not adequately developing its social function in relation to education, both in terms of encouraging the population to go to university and in providing sufficient means and resources to welcome students into higher education.

Article 205 of the Federal Constitution (BRASIL, 1988a), transcribed below, pays special attention to education.

> Article 205. Education, the right of all and the duty of the State and the family, shall be promoted and encouraged with the collaboration of society, with a view to the full development of the person, their preparation for the exercise of citizenship and their qualification for work. (emphasis added)

The National Education Guidelines and Bases Law, Law No. 9.394 (BRASIL, 1996c), establishes the guidelines and bases of national education, stating in its second article:

> Art. 2: Education, a duty of the family and the State, inspired by the principles of freedom and the ideals of human solidarity, has as its purpose the full development of the student, his preparation for the exercise of citizenship and his

qualification for work.

From the above, it has been understood that it is the duty of the state to offer education to the people. In an attempt to comply with this constitutional and legal premise, Law No. 11.096 (BRASIL, 2005a) was published, which instituted the University for All Program (PROUNI), aimed at increasing the number of places at universities, democratizing access to them for people in need and investing in the quality of teaching.

3.1 Fundamentals

PROUNI is a program created by the Federal Government and administered by the Ministry of Education (MEC), which offers full or partial scholarships of (50%) (fifty percent) or 25% (twenty-five percent) at private for-profit or non-profit higher education institutions. The Program was created by Provisional Measure No. 213 (BRASIL, 2004d), and converted into Law No. 11.096 (BRASIL, 2005a), with the aim of encouraging Brazilians considered to be economically disadvantaged to enter higher education. It is considered by the Ministry of Education (MEC) to be the largest scholarship program in the history of Brazilian education, as it aims to direct more than three hundred thousand young people and teachers from the public sector to private universities.

According to data provided by the Ministry of Education, in its first selection process (2005), PROUNI offered one hundred and twelve thousand scholarships at 1,142 higher education institutions across the country. Over the next four years, the program plans to offer four hundred thousand new scholarships. All these actions are in line with the goals of the National Education Plan, which foresees the presence, by 2010, of at least 30% (thirty percent) of the population aged between 18 and 24 in higher education, currently restricted to 10.4% (ten and a quarter percent).

Today, the program is already being recognized internationally, as reported in the American magazine *Higher Education* (2007): "*Program Prouni: Changing the panorama of Access to Higher Education in Brazil. Although more than 4,000,000 students are enrolled in higher education in Brazil, only 11% of the young people in the range of 18 to 24 years attend higher education schools.*"

The National Institute for Educational Studies and Research Anisio Teixeira (2007) reported that in 2006, the private higher education institutions in the state of Ceará linked to PROUNI offered 1,847 scholarships, of which 1,493 were full scholarships and 354 were partial scholarships.

In the document "Information for applicants", the MEC (2006) defines a scholarship as a benefit granted to the student in the form of a partial or full discount on the fees charged by private educational institutions.

To be eligible for a full scholarship, the student's per capita family income (per person in the family) cannot exceed one and a half minimum wages in force in the country. The partial scholarship of fifty percent (50%) can be granted to students with a per capita family income of no more than three minimum wages. The twenty-five percent (25%) partial scholarship will be awarded to students with a family income per person of up to three minimum wages, only for courses with a monthly fee of up to R$ 200.00 (two hundred reais).

Nature of the grant	Family Income
Full scholarship	≤ 1.5 minimum wages
Partial scholarship	> 1.5 minimum wages and ≤ 3 minimum wages

TABLE 3 - Scholarships x *per capita* family income

Source: Own elaboration.

According to Law No. 11.096 (BRASIL, 2005a), a family group is defined as, in addition to the applicant themselves, the group of people living in the applicant's household, who receive the monthly family income and who are related to the applicant by the following degrees of kinship: father, stepfather, stepmother, spouse, partner, child, stepchild, sibling, grandparent.

Article 2 of the law states that the Brazilians who can benefit from the program are the following:

a) students who have attended secondary school in public schools or private schools on a full scholarship;

b) students with special needs, under the terms of the law,

c) have attended secondary school partially in a public school and partially in a private institution, as a full scholarship student of the respective institution, and

d) be a teacher in the public school system, in full time employment, as part of the permanent staff of the institution and applying for places on degree courses, higher education normal or pedagogy. In this case, family income per person is not taken into account.

To take part in the selection process, students must have taken part in the 2006 National High School Exam (ENEM) and obtained a minimum score of 45 points (arithmetic average of the essay and general knowledge tests), as established by the Ministry of Education. Scores obtained in previous ENEMs are not taken into account. The ENEM results are used as a criterion for the distribution of scholarships, i.e. the scholarships are distributed according to the marks obtained by the students in the ENEM. Thus, the students who achieve the best marks in the exam will have a better chance of choosing the course and institution where they will study.

The selection will therefore be made in two stages. In the first, the results and socio-economic profile of the ENEM (National High School Exam) will be analyzed. In the second, the educational institution itself, at its discretion, will define the form of selection, at no cost to the competing student, as determined by article 4 of Decree 5.493 (BRASIL, 2005d).

In addition to the interview, the selection criterion of the institution being researched is participation in the entrance exam held by the institution itself, and the result will not be eliminatory, but only classificatory.

3.2 Joining the program

Article 5 of the aforementioned Law 11.096 (BRASIL, 2005a) states that in order to join the program, Private Higher Education Institutions (with or without non-charitable purposes) must sign an agreement with the Ministry of Education, which will be valid for 10 (ten) years from the date the agreement is signed, committing themselves to offering at least 1 (one) full scholarship to the equivalent of 10.7 (ten whole and seven tenths) paying students regularly enrolled in their undergraduate courses.

Table 5 shows a random example to clarify what the law says.

Suppose that a particular private higher education institution, referred to here as "X", wants to join PROUNI in 2006 and wants to know how many full-tuition places it must commit to offering. It is known, therefore, that Institution "X" has 2,000 students regularly enrolled, distributed between the Law, Accountancy and IT courses.

TABLE 5 - Adhesion to PROUNI - Number of full scholarships to be offered in the selection process

Course	I No. of paying students	Full scholarships
Law	1.000	94
Accounting	700	65
Computer Science	300	28
Total	**2.000**	**187**

Source: Own elaboration

The law stipulates that for every 10.7 students regularly enrolled, the institution must offer a full scholarship. In the example above, as Institution "X" has 2,000 (two thousand) students, it must offer at least 187 full scholarships in order to join PROUNI. Of these, 94 must be allocated to the Law course, 65 to the Accountancy course and 28 to the IT course.

Article 9(I) of MEC Ordinance 1.704 (BRASIL, 2006c) states that the formula to be used to calculate full scholarships is as follows:

$$I = \frac{X}{10,7}$$

Where, I = the total number of full scholarships to be offered in the selection process and X = the number of regularly paying students enrolled at the end of the semester.

3.2.1 Disengagement from the Adhesion Agreement

The educational institution may choose to withdraw from the agreement. This measure will not entail any burden for the Government, nor for the student who has benefited from it, who will enjoy the benefit until the end of their course.

The tax rule also stipulates that if there is an imbalance in the proportion informed in the agreement, the institution must re-establish this proportion by offering new scholarships at each selection process.

3.3 Exchange of Scholarships between Courses and Shifts

The Adhesion Agreement may also provide for the exchange of scholarships between courses and shifts, restricted to 1/5 (one fifth) of the scholarships offered for each course and each shift. In the example above, of the total number of scholarships for the Law course, nineteen (19) could be transferred to the other courses, thirteen (13) scholarships could be transferred to the Accountancy course, and only five (5) scholarships could be transferred to the other courses for the Informatics course.

3.3.1 Full, Partial and Permanent Bursaries

Alternatively, as a substitute for offering a full scholarship for every 10.7 students enrolled, institutions that adhere to PROUNI may offer one (1) full scholarship for every 22 (twenty-two) regularly paying students duly enrolled on courses actually held at the institution, must additionally offer partial scholarships of 50% (fifty percent) or 25% (twenty-five percent) in the proportion necessary for the sum of the benefits granted in accordance with the Law to reach the equivalent of 8.5% (eight integers and five tenths percent) of the annual revenue actually received is what Art. 5 of Law 11.096 (BRASIL, 2005a).

In this case, following the example described above, instead of offering one hundred and eighty-seven (187) full scholarships, only ninety-one (91) would be offered. However, the institution that chooses to do so must also offer partial scholarships of 50% (fifty percent) or 25% (twenty-five percent). The total number of scholarships offered (full and partial) must reach 8.5% (eight and a half percent) of the annual income (semester and yearly fees).

Item II of Article 9 of Ordinance No. 1.704 (BRASIL, 2006c) shows the formulas that should be used for this situation:

$I = \frac{X}{22}$, for calculating the number of full scholarships, and

$P = \frac{V}{\left(SM/2\right)}$, for calculating the number of partial grants, where:

Where,

I = total number of full scholarships to be offered in the selection process;

X = number of regularly paying students enrolled at the end of the semester;

P = number of 50% partial scholarships to be offered in the selection process;

V = value of the estimated base revenue available for offering 50% partial scholarships in the selection process;

SM = average semester fee = estimated average monthly fee for the semester multiplied by 6;

R = base income for calculating the number of scholarships to be offered in the selection process for the semester;

VI = the amount corresponding to the full scholarships still in use and suspended from previous semesters and the full scholarships to be offered in the following semester.

Article 5 of Decree 5.493 (BRASIL, 2005d) - the PROUNI Regulation - clarifies that regular paying students are those who have signed an onerous contract with a higher education institution based on Law 9.870 (BRASIL, 1999a).

(BRASIL, 1999a), who are not beneficiaries of full PROUNI scholarships from the institution itself, excluding those in default for more than 90 (ninety) days, whose enrollment has been refused in the academic period immediately following the default.

According to MEC Decrees 4 (BRASIL, 2006a) and 1556 (BRASIL, 2006b), the scholarship may be terminated or suspended in the following situations:

a) termination of the scholarship:

- the beneficiary student has not enrolled in the academic period corresponding to the first semester of the scholarship;

- termination of the enrolment of the beneficiary student, with the consequent termination of the respective academic links with the institution;

- enrollment of the scholarship holder, at any time, in a free public higher education institution;

- completion of the course in which the student is the beneficiary of the scholarship or any other higher education course at any higher education institution;

- insufficient academic performance, and the ProUni coordinator, after hearing the person(s) responsible for the subject(s) in which the student failed, may authorize, once only, the continuation of the scholarship;

- at any time, if a document presented or information provided by the scholarship holder is incorrect, under the terms of §1 of art. 1 of Decree 5.493 (BRASIL, 2005d);

- expiry of the maximum time limit for completion of the respective degree course or specific training sequence;

- failure to update after three consecutive semesters of suspension;

- a substantial change in the scholar's socio-economic condition which compromises compliance with the requirements set out in §§ 1 and 2 of Article 1 of Law No. 11.096 (BRASIL, 2005a);

- in the event that the scholarship recipient simultaneously uses the scholarship granted by ProUni and financing granted under the Higher Education Student Financing Fund - FIES, in different courses or educational institutions;

- request by the scholar; court decision or order; evasion of the scholar; and death of the scholar.

b) suspension of scholarship:

- not updated in the specified period;

- in the case of partial scholarship holders whose enrollment has been refused due to default on the portion of the tuition fee for which they are responsible, in accordance with the provisions of Law No. 9,870 (BRASIL, 1999a);

- in the event of the beneficiary student suspending enrolment or abandoning the academic period;

- in the event of a class not being formed in the initial academic period of the course or qualification, exclusively for scholarship recipients in the selection process for the first semester of 2005.

- Each suspension may not exceed three consecutive semesters, under penalty of termination of the scholarship.

The Permanence Scholarship is a monthly benefit of R$ 300.00 (three hundred reais), granted to students with a full scholarship.

(three hundred reais) per month, granted to students with a full scholarship in use, enrolled in face-to-face courses of at least 6 (six) semesters' duration and whose average workload is greater than or equal to 6 (six) class hours per day.

This average workload is calculated by the quotient between the minimum total workload of the course, in hours, and the product obtained by multiplying the respective minimum period in years for completing the course and the number of days in the school year, which is set by the National

Education Guidelines and Bases Law - LDB (BRASIL, 1996c) at 200 (two hundred) school days.

3.3.2 PROUNI System - SISPROUNI

SISPROUNI is the electronic system made available by the MEC, through which Private Higher Education Institutions transmit the Adhesion Agreement via the internet. [All operational procedures relating to PROUNI membership will be carried out exclusively through SISPROUNI, and their validity is conditional on a digital signature].

In addition to guaranteeing total security for the information registered on SISPROUNI, the use of digital certification makes it possible to register a digital signature on all documents issued, which means that they don't have to be sent by post, nor do they have to be notarized. The legal validity of these documents is guaranteed by Provisional Measure 2.200-2 (BRASIL, 2001a).

According to data published by the MEC (2007) in the document "PROUNI wins quality award in Education", SISPROUNI received 1.7 million queries from students in the second selection process of 2007, with an average connection and registration time of ten minutes. The system was also able to allow simultaneous access by 53,000 people, as well as enrolling 103,521 students in PROUNI in a single day.

3.4 Obligations of the Educational Institution and Academic Performance Requirements

Art. 7 of Law No. 11.096 (BRASIL, 2005a) lays down certain obligations to which the Institutions must comply, under penalty of losing the rights provided for in the law:

Art. 7 [...]

I - the proportion of scholarships offered per course, shift and unit, respecting the parameters established in Article 5 of this Law;

II - percentage of scholarships earmarked for the implementation of affirmative policies for access to higher education for people with disabilities or self-declared indigenous and black people.

§ 1 ° The percentage referred to in item II of the *caput of* this article must be at least equal to the percentage of self-declared indigenous, brown or black citizens in the respective unit of the Federation, according to the last census of the Brazilian Institute of Geography and Statistics - IBGE.

§ 2 ° [...]

§ 3 ° [...]

§ 4 The Ministry of Education will withdraw from Prouni a course considered insufficient, without prejudice to the student already enrolled, according to the performance criteria of the National Higher Education Evaluation System - SINAES, for 3 (three) consecutive evaluations, in which case the scholarships for the withdrawn course, in the following selection processes, will have to be redistributed proportionally among the other courses of the institution, respecting the provisions of art. 5 of this Law.

In accordance with the provisions of art. 14 of Decree 5.493 (BRASIL, 2005d), the Higher Education Institution that joins PROUNI will submit to the Ministry of Education, annually or every semester, according to the respective academic curriculum:

a) control of the scholarship holder's compulsory minimum attendance, corresponding to 75% (seventy-five percent) of the course load;

b) the scholarship holder's progress in the course, with particular regard to academic performance, and

c) the dropout rate of students by course and shift, as well as the total number of students enrolled, including students linked to PROUNI.

According to Article 5 of Ordinance No. 1.704 (BRASIL, 2006c), it is still up to the Private Higher Education Institution:

a) consider, in scholarships offered through the regular selection process, all educational costs, including enrollment and those related to subjects taken as a result of failure, observing the requirements of the scholar's academic performance;

b) refrain from charging any kind of fees in the selection process;

c) provide access to the internet for candidates to register for the selection process; d) inform the public of the number of full or partial scholarships on offer.

With regard to the student linked to PROUNI, beneficiary of a full or partial scholarship, they must show academic success in at least 75% (seventy-five percent) of the subjects taken in each academic term. In the event of insufficient academic performance, the PROUNI coordinator, after hearing the person(s) responsible for the subject(s) in which the student failed, may authorize the continuation of the scholarship on a one-off basis.

3.4.1 Performance evaluation

One of the criteria for remaining in PROUNI is that institutions maintain sufficient performance in the National Higher Education Evaluation System - SINAES.

According to §4 of the above-mentioned legislation, under the SINAES system, the evaluation will be divided into three areas, which will be evaluated in three consecutive years, one in each year. After the first round, if there is a bad evaluation, the institution will sign a commitment to correct the deficiencies and improve as SINAES and, only after having passed the second round of exams in each area, can any punishment be applied, without prejudice to the student already enrolled.

3.5 Tax exemption

Private Higher Education Institutions, whether for-profit or not-for-profit, which adhere to PROUNI under the terms of Law 11.096 (BRASIL, 2005a), are exempt from IRPJ and CSLL (which are levied on operating profits) and PIS and COFINS (which are levied on turnover) for the duration of the Adhesion Agreement.

Not included in the scope of the benefit is PASEP, whose contributors are The Union, the States, the Municipalities, the Federal District and the Territories; the autarchies, public companies, mixed-capital companies and foundations, of the Union, the States, the Municipalities, the Federal District and the Territories, in accordance with Complementary Law No. 8 (BRASIL, 1970b).

According to article 10 of Law 9.718 (BRASIL, 1998c), a non-profit organization is one that does not have a surplus in its accounts or, if it does in a given year, allocates this profit entirely to the maintenance and development of its social objectives. Whereas for-profit entities aim exclusively for a surplus.

Non-profit organizations include private community, confessional and philanthropic institutions, which, according to the definitions in the glossary of the Higher Education Census published by INEP (2006), consist of:

> Private Community Institutions are set up by one or more legal entities, including teachers' and students' cooperatives, which include a representative of the community in their founding body. Private community HEIs are part of the Federal Higher Education System and are therefore supervised by the federal government;
>
> Confessional private institution - set up by groups of individuals or by one or more legal entities which follow a specific confessional and ideological orientation and which include a representative of the faith in their founding body. Confessional private HEIs are part of the Federal Higher Education System and are therefore supervised by the federal government.
>
> Private philanthropic institution - in accordance with the law, this is an educational or social assistance institution that provides the services for which it was established and makes them available to the general population, in a complementary manner to the activities of the State, without any remuneration. Private philanthropic HEIs are part of the Federal Higher Education System and are therefore supervised by the federal government.

The exemption now granted by the legislation applies only to the revenue from exempt activities (revenue exclusive to the undergraduate activity), whether in the case of exemptions on profit or on billing. Therefore, institutions with multiple activities must segregate exempt activities in their books.

3.5.1 Tax regime for private institutions

There is currently a difference in the tax regime between for-profit and non-profit institutions. For-profit entities pay all the taxes related to PROUNI, which are IRPJ, CSLL, PIS and COFINS, while non-profit entities only pay PIS calculated on the payroll and, in some cases, COFINS. PROUNI will allow for isonomic tax treatment of private higher education institutions.

Table 4 shows the difference in the incidence of taxes due by institutional category, then compares for-profit, non-profit (confessional and community) and philanthropic institutions, before and after joining PROUNI. The calculation basis and rates of the main federal taxes in the three categories of private establishments are broken down.

Taxes due	Calculation base and rate					
			Non-profit institutions			
	For-profit institutions		Confessional/community		Philanthropic	
	Normal	With PROUNI	Normal	With PROUNI	Normal	With PROUNI
IRPJ	25% of profit	-	-	-	-	-
CSLL	9% of profit	-	-	-	-	-
COFINS	3% of revenue - tuition fees received		3% of revenue - tuition fees received			
PIS	0.65% of revenue - tuition received	-	1% of payroll	-	1% on payroll	-

TABLE 4 - Main taxes due by HEI category

Source: Carvalho (2006).

Table 4 shows a comparison of the taxes owed by private higher education institutions (IRPJ, CSLL, COFINS and PIS) and which will be exempt from paying them if they opt to join PROUNI. It also presents the same comparison between the taxes owed by non-profit institutions that join PROUNI or not.

3.5.2 Operating Profit - Basis for Calculating the Exemption

On October 8, 2004, the Federal Revenue Office published Normative Instruction 456 (BRASIL, 2004a), which defines the rules for determining the amounts of the tax benefit.

The exemption will apply to operating profit in relation to IRPJ and CSLL, and to revenue earned exclusively from higher education activities, in relation to PIS and COFINS.

Operating profit, in accordance with article 544 of the Income Tax Regulations and article 2 of Normative Instruction SRF 456 (BRASIL, 2004a) is the net profit for the accounting period, before deduction of the provision for CSLL and the provision for income tax, adjusted by the exclusion of the following amounts:

I - the part of financial income that exceeds financial expenses;

II - income and losses from shareholdings;

III - non-operating results; and

IV - the amount written off the revaluation reserve, in cases where the realized value of the assets subject to the revaluation has been recorded as an operating cost or expense and the write-off of the reserve has been made against a non-operating income or net equity account, not computed in the result for the same period.

The above is summarized in Table 5 below.

Taxes	Exemption on
COFINS	Monthly revenue
PIS	Monthly revenue
CSLL	Operating profit
IRPJ	Operating profit

TABLE 5 - Basis for calculating tax exemptions

Source: Azevedo and Senne (2006, p. 387).

According to art. 3 of Normative Instruction 456 (BRASIL, 2004a), in order to benefit from the exemption, the Private Higher Education Institution must clearly and accurately demonstrate in its accounts the elements that make up the income, costs, expenses and results for the period of calculation, relating to the activities on which the exemption falls, segregated from other activities.

If the accounting system adopted by the educational institution does not offer the necessary conditions for calculating net income and operating profit by activity, the institution may establish the calculation basis based on the ratio between net income from exempt activities and total net income.

Article *4 of the* aforementioned Normative Instruction states that the following are grounds for losing the benefit, in the calendar year corresponding to the exemption benefit: committing acts that constitute crimes against the tax order, and failing to issue invoices.

The granting or recognition of the tax benefit is conditional on the taxpayer proving to the Federal Revenue Office that they have paid their taxes in full.

Failure to comply with any of the obligations assumed in the Adhesion Agreement will subject the Educational Institution to disconnection from PROUNI and, consequently, to the suspension of the tax benefit.

3.6 Penalties

Article 9 of Law 11.096 (BRASIL, 2005a) stipulates that failure to comply with

of the obligations assumed in the accession agreement will subject the institutions to the following penalties:

I - re-establishment of the number of scholarships to be offered free of charge, which will be determined, at each selection process, whenever the institution fails to comply with the percentage established in art. 5 of this Law and which must be sufficient to maintain the percentage established therein, with an increase of 1/5 (one fifth);

II - disconnection from Prouni, determined in the event of a repeat offence, in the event of serious misconduct, in accordance with the regulations, without prejudice to the students benefiting from the program and at no cost to the public authorities.

§ 1 The penalties provided for in the *caput of* this article will be applied by the Ministry of Education, under the terms of the regulations, after an administrative procedure has been set up, with the right to an adversarial hearing and the right of defense assured.

PROUNI legislation considers what is referred to in item II above to be serious misconduct, specifying it as follows:

a) repeated non-compliance with the infraction referred to in item I of art.

9, ascertained in a prior administrative process (inspection);

b) discriminatory treatment between paying students and PROUNI beneficiaries, and

c) misrepresentation in the information provided in the adhesion agreement, in order to unduly broaden the scope of the tax benefits provided by PROUNI.

3.7 Current Scenario: In Brazil, Ceará and the Researched Institution.

The results of PROUNI in Brazil, according to MEC data, are quite satisfactory. At the end of 2006, PROUNI offered 108,642 scholarships to 517,748 students. One of the selection criteria was the student's ENEM score. In 2006, the states of the North and Northeast regions stood out, achieving the best averages in the exam. Ceará was the best performer nationally, with an average of 68.44 points, followed by Pernambuco, with 68.3, and Parà, with 67.46. The national average was 62.73 points, bearing in mind that the minimum score to take part in the program is 45 points.

The top placings, according to the MEC, show that the most competitive courses are also receiving scholarships. Of the 30 best-placed students, 17 are studying medicine, 3 engineering, 3 law, 2 psychology and 1 each for veterinary, design, architecture, information systems technology and accounting.

Students in the University for All Program (ProUni) achieved averages equal to or higher than their peers in the 14 areas of knowledge assessed by the National Institute of Educational Studies and Research Anisio Teixeira (Inep) in 2006.

29,098 places were offered under the quota system and for the first time the overall average of quota students, which was 62.82 points, exceeded the overall average (62.62). Of the 108,642 scholarships offered, 45.8% (forty-five and eight-hundredths percent) were taken up by black students. Teachers of primary school pupils took up 1,474 places; the disabled occupied 423 and 63 were designated for indigenous people.

The grants awarded in 2005 and 2006 now total 204,249. Of these, 167,437 are studying regularly and 1,126 have already graduated. The remainder is made up of students who no longer use the scholarship because they have better economic conditions, obtained another type of scholarship, dropped out, died, lost the benefit by court order or for other reasons.

In an interview with the PROUNI coordinator and the coordinator of the accounting course at "Instituiçao Construir", it was reported that the PROUNI students are really dedicated and studious, and that there have been no dropouts on the part of these students.

Students who had benefited from the program were also interviewed. The results obtained are surprising, both in terms of learning and the social aspect. The students are easily entering the job market and, as a result, generating the financial resources needed to cover any expenses incurred with their studies, as well as helping their families. Many of them moved from the interior of the state to enter university through PRONI and are already supporting themselves with the salaries/scholarships they receive.

It's worth noting that the Construir institution has a system of support for students who have received PROUNI scholarships to take up internships in public and private companies, which has contributed to the fact that all the students who have received them are being paid.

This chapter deals with the operating rules of PROUNI, which are regulated by Law 11.096 (BRASIL, 2005a) and complementary legislation. The nature and characteristics of the taxes from which private institutions are exempt as a result of joining PROUNI are discussed in the following chapter.

4 TAXES RELATED TO PROUNI

Article 8 of Law 11.096 (BRASIL, 2005a), which instituted the University for All Program (PROUNI), exempts Higher Education Institutions (for-profit or not-for-profit) that join the program from the following taxes: Corporate Income Tax (IRPJ); Social Contribution on Net Profits (CSLL); Social Contribution for Social Security Financing (COFINS), and Contribution to the Social Integration Program (PIS).

The taxes listed here will be briefly commented on, covering: concepts, jurisdiction, taxable event, basis of calculation, rates, taxpayers, exemptions, etc.

4.1 Corporate Income Tax (IRPJ)

Income tax was instituted by article 153, III, of the Federal Constitution (BRASIL, 1988a). In the National Tax Code (CTN) (BRASIL, 1966), Income Tax is dealt with in articles 43, 44 and 45 and in ordinary legislation there are numerous laws, decree-laws and provisional measures that regulate this tax. These laws are consolidated in the Income Tax Regulation - RIR.

4.1.1 Competence

According to article 153, III of the Federal Constitution (BRASIL, 1988a), and article 43 of the CTN, the Union is responsible for instituting income tax.

According to Machado (2000 p. 39):

> The creation and collection of such a tax has been attributed to the Union for two reasons. Firstly, because through it, the Union is able to redistribute income between different regions of the country, applying resources from the tax collected in the South and Southeast to the Northeast, for example. Secondly, because the distribution of taxpayers' wealth throughout the national territory could make it very difficult or even impossible for states and municipalities to collect this tax, creating numerous conflicts of jurisdiction.

According to surveys carried out by the Federal Revenue Service (SRF) (2007), in 2006 the country collected R$56,175,887,178 (fifty-six billion, one hundred and seventy-five million, eight hundred and eighty-seven thousand, one hundred and seventy-eight reais) in IRPJ. Of this total, the state of Ceará contributed R$493,230,851 (four hundred and ninety-three million, two hundred and thirty thousand, eight hundred and fifty-one reais), or approximately eighty-eight hundredths of a percent (0.88%). It is not known for certain, perhaps due to a lack of disclosure, how the amount collected was distributed by region.

4.1.2 Taxable event

Income tax is levied on income or earnings of any kind. The National Tax Code, seeking to make the constitutional precept explicit, clarified that the taxable event of this tax is the acquisition of economic or legal availability of income or proceeds of any nature.

According to Latorraca (1999, p. 104), the concept of income, which includes earnings, includes: the product of capital, labor or a combination of both. Thus, the tax obligation arises when the legal entity acquires legal or economic availability of the income, i.e. when there is an increase in assets.

4.1.3 Basis of calculation

According to article 44 of the CTN (BRAZIL, 1966), the basis for calculating Corporate Income Tax is real, presumed or arbitrated profit.

Real profit is the net accounting profit calculated in the commercial bookkeeping, adjusted by additions and exclusions or compensations authorized by tax legislation, as set out in article 247 of Decree 3,000 (BRASIL, 1999b).

The Real Profit is found in the Statement transcribed in Part 'A' of the Real Profit Calculation Book (LALUR), diagrammed in Table 6:

Net profit for the calculation period, before income tax
(+) Additions
(-) Exclusions
Subtotal
(-) Offsetting Tax Losses
(=) Actual Profit

TABLE 6 - Statement of the calculation of Real Profit

Source: Own elaboration.

If there are exclusions with an absolute value greater than the sum of the other parts, even starting from a profit, a Tax Loss will be calculated and, therefore, there will be no income tax to provision for in the accounts and to pay, however, if the accounting result is a loss, but there are additions with values greater than the sum of the other parts, a Real Profit will be calculated and, therefore, it is appropriate to provision for and pay income tax.

Offsets represent accumulated tax losses recorded in part 'B' of the Real Profit Calculation Book (LALUR). Article 5 of Law 9.065 (BRASIL, 1995b) states that tax losses can only reduce the Real Profit already adjusted for additions and exclusions by a maximum of thirty percent (30%).

Presumed profit is an optional and simplified way of calculating profit and, consequently, corporate income tax. However, it is restricted to taxpayers who are not obliged to calculate on the basis of real profit. Presumed profit is determined by applying a specific percentage to the gross revenue earned in the activity.

Arbitrated profit is determined by the tax authorities for calculating income tax, when the legal entity fails to comply with accessory obligations relating to the determination of actual or presumed profit or refuses to provide accounting and tax books and documents requested by the tax authorities.

According to Oliveira, Chieregato (2003, p.174) arbitrated profit is:

> a resource used by the tax authorities, almost always as a last resort, which should only be applied when there is an absolute lack of confidence in the taxpayer's bookkeeping, due to the lack or insufficiency of concrete elements that allow the identification or verification of the calculation basis used in taxation by real or presumed profit. It can also be used by the tax authorities in cases where the taxpayer refuses or hinders the tax authority's access to supporting documentation.

Figure 1 summarizes the types of taxation provided for in the CTN and the respective income tax assessment system determined by Article 2, Paragraph 3 of Law No. 9430.

(BRASIL, 1966).

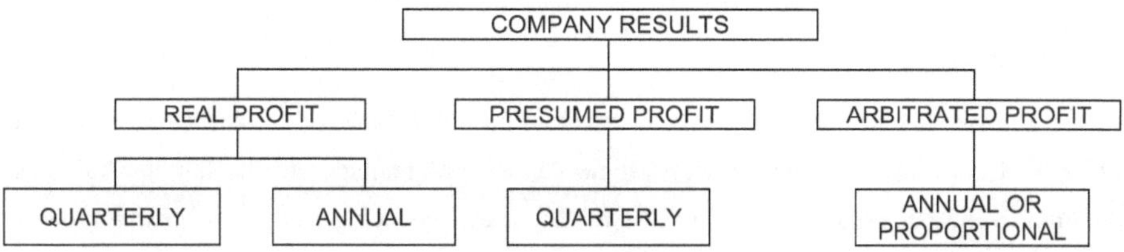

FIGURE 1 - Types of taxation and Income Tax Calculation System Source: Own elaboration.

Companies taxed on the real profit basis may calculate income tax based on the profit for the year (annual calculation) or based on the profit calculated each quarter (calculations on March 31, June 30, September 30 and December 31). In the case of annual assessment, the company is obliged to pay the IRPJ calculated on a monthly basis based on estimates (calculated on gross revenue or through profits calculated in tax reduction or suspension balance sheets), which will be deducted from the amount due for the year.

Companies taxed on the basis of Presumed Profit calculate IRPJ on a quarterly basis, which will be levied on all their revenue. In the case of Arbitrated Profit, the tax authorities define the IRPJ assessment period.

The Private Higher Education Institution surveyed calculated IRPJ based on annual real profit, taking the reduction or suspension balance sheets as the monthly calculation basis, for the period from January 2005 to June 2006.

For the purposes of calculating the PROUNI exemption, the exempt income tax is levied on the operating profit, understood as the net profit for the calculation period before the CSLL provision and the IRPJ provision have been computed, adjusted by the exclusions provided for in Article 2 of Normative Instruction SRF No. 456 (BRASIL, 2004a), as shown in Table 7. The amount of exempt income tax calculated on the basis of operating profit will be deducted from the income tax due on the basis of real profit.

IRPJ calculation base (PROUNI)= Operating profit

Operating Profit= Net Profit before IRPJ/CSLL provisions - Exclusions

TABLE 7 - Determination of Operating Profit

Source: Own elaboration.

4.1.4 Rate

Legal entities have their profits taxed at a rate of 15% (fifteen percent), which may be increased by an additional 10% (ten percent) on the portion of the monthly profit that exceeds twenty thousand reais, in accordance with article 3 of Law 9.249 (BRASIL, 1995c).

4.1.5 Taxpayer

The legal concept of income tax payer is set out in article 45 of the CTN: "Taxpayer of the tax is the holder of the availability referred to in article 43, without prejudice to the law attributing this condition to the possessor, in any capacity, of the assets producing income or taxable proceeds" (BRASIL, 1966). The IRPJ taxpayer is, therefore, the legal entity or equivalent, which has earned income, profits and earnings.

4.1.6 Exemption from IRPJ

The following entities are exempt from IRPJ:

a) philanthropic, recreational, cultural and non-profit civil associations, all based on Articles 15 and 18 of Law No. 9,532; (BRASIL, 1997b);

b) higher education institutions that have joined the University for All Program (PROUNI), subject to the provisions of Law 11.096; (BRASIL, 2004a);

c) closed private pension funds and non-profit organizations, in accordance with article 175 of Decree 3.000 - RIR/99; (BRASIL, 1999b);

d) foreign transportation companies, in accordance with article 176 of Decree 3.000 - RIR/99; (BRASIL, 1999b);

e) Savings and loan associations, according to article 177 of Decree No. 3000 - RIR/99, and (BRASIL, 1999b), and

f) Investment companies, as provided for in article 178 of Decree No. 3000 - RIR/99. (BRASIL, 1999b).

The following are subject to specific exemptions:

g) the Itaipu Binational Entity, according to article 180 of the RIR/99 (BRASIL, 1999b), and

h) the Fundo Garantidor de Crédito - FGC (Credit Guarantee Fund), provided for in article 4 of Law 9.710 (BRASIL, 1998a).

Normally, the exemption is granted by the State to meet the social and economic interests of the region, sector or country. In the cases listed here, the payment of IRPJ is waived in order to encourage certain activities, stimulate the social growth of non-profit organizations and indirectly develop their social function (as is the case with PROUNI).

4.2 Social Contribution on Net Profits (CSLL)

The social contribution on net profit (CSLL) is a source of funds provided for in Article 195, Item I of the Federal Constitution to meet the social security program. It was instituted by Law No. 7.689 (BRASIL, 1988b), later amended by Laws Nos. 8.981 (BRASIL, 1995a), 9.065 (BRASIL, 1999b) and 9.430 (BRASIL, 1996d) and consolidated by SRF Normative Instruction No. 390 (BRASIL, 2004b).

According to data provided by the Federal Revenue Secretariat (SRF), the total CSLL collected in Brazil in 2006 and which must be passed on to maintain social security was R$ 28,316,301,431 (twenty-eight billion, three hundred and sixteen million, three hundred and one thousand, four hundred and thirty-one reais). The State of Ceará's share of total revenue was one whole nine hundredths of a percent (1.09%), corresponding to R$ 311,162,276 (three hundred and eleven million, one hundred and sixty-two thousand, two hundred and seventy-six thousand).

This is a social contribution under the jurisdiction of the Union, as set out in article 149 of the Federal Constitution. (BRAZIL, 1988a), whose taxpayers are legal entities domiciled in the country and those equated to them by income tax legislation.

According to Law No. 7.689 (BRASIL, 1988b), the same rules apply to the calculation and payment of CSLL as those established for corporate income tax, thus maintaining the calculation basis and rates laid down in the specific legislation in force. Thus, the taxable event, calculation, payment date and taxpayers of CSLL are similar to those determined for IRPJ.

4.2.1 Basis of calculation

As with income tax, CSLL is calculated on a quarterly or annual real, presumed or arbitrated basis.

The basis for calculating CSLL for legal entities that calculate income tax based on real profit was defined in Article 2 of Law No. 7.689 (BRASIL, 1988b), as the amount of the result for the year (accounting profit), before the provision for IRPJ, adjusted by the additions, exclusions and deductions provided for by law, as shown in Table 8.

Net profit or loss for the period, before calculating the IRPJ provision
(+) Additions
(-) Exclusions
Subtotal
(-) Negative tax base from previous periods
(=) Social Contribution on Profit calculation basis

TABLE 8 - Statement of the calculation of the Social Contribution on Net Profit base

Source: Own elaboration.

The net profit (subtotal), after being adjusted by the additions and exclusions prescribed or authorized by CSLL legislation, may be reduced by the offsetting of negative tax bases from previous calculation periods, by up to a maximum of thirty percent (30%) of said adjusted profit, as set out in articles 12 and 16 of Law 9.065 (BRASIL, 1995b).

The institution being researched calculates CSLL based on Real Profit, a monthly estimate based on the suspension/reduction balance sheets and, for the purposes of calculating the PROUNI exemption, the Social Contribution will be levied on operating profit, understood as net profit for the calculation period before the provision for CSLL and the provision for IR have been computed, adjusted by the exclusions provided for in Article 2 of SRF Normative Instruction no. 456 (BRASILIA, 2004a). 456 (BRASIL, 2004a).

4.2.2 Rate

The CSLL rates, which represent the percentages that will be applied to the calculated tax base (profit), have undergone some changes since they were created (1988). Currently, under the terms of article 37 of Law 10.637 (BRASIL, 2002a), the CSLL is determined by applying a rate of 9% (nine percent) to the adjusted net profit. The rate to be considered by financial institutions, according to Law No. 9.316 (BRASIL, 1996a), is eighteen percent (18%).

4.2.3 CSLL exemption

The following institutions are exempt from CSLL:

a) philanthropic, recreational, cultural and non-profit civil associations, all based on Articles 15 and 18 of Law No. 9532 (BRASIL, 1997b), and

b) higher education institutions that have joined the University for All Program (PROUNI), subject to the provisions of Law 11.096 (BRASIL, 2004a).

There are also some specific exemptions:

a) the Itaipu binational entity, as provided for in article 180 of Decree No. 3,000 (BRASIL, 1999b);

b) closed supplementary pension entities, as set out in Article 4 of Law No. 6.435 (BRAZIL, 1977);

c) cooperative societies, with the exception of consumer societies, in accordance with articles 39 and 46 of Law 10.865 (BRASIL, 2004a).

As with the IRPJ, the federal government grants exemption from the CSLL tax in order to serve the country's economic and social interests. In order to develop its social function, the state benefits private higher education institutions that join PROUNI by waiving these taxes.

4.3 Social Integration Program (PIS)

The contribution to the Social Integration Program (PIS) was instituted by Complementary Law No. 7 (BRASIL, 1970a), accepted by art. 239 of the Federal Constitution. (BRASIL, 1988a), intended to fund unemployment insurance and a bonus of one minimum wage per year for employees earning up to two minimum wages who participate in the program.

The amount of PIS collected in the country in 2006, which must be passed on to taxpayers to pay unemployment insurance and salary bonuses, was R$24,276,526,065 (twenty-four billion, two hundred and seventy-six million, five hundred and twenty-six thousand, sixty-five reais), according to data provided by the Federal Revenue Office (SRF). Of the total collected, the state of Ceará contributed R$342,009,252 (three hundred and forty-two million, nine thousand, two hundred and fifty-two reais), corresponding to one whole forty-one hundredth of a percent (1.41%).

4.3.1 Tax Jurisdiction

According to Article 149 of the Federal Constitution (BRASIL, 1988a), the Union has the power to institute and collect the PIS contribution.

4.3.2 Taxpayer

The PIS contribution is payable monthly by legal entities governed by private law and those treated as such by income tax legislation, by non-profit entities, foundations, cooperative societies and financial institutions, with the exception of Micro-enterprises (ME) and Small Businesses (EPP), which are subject to the Simples Nacional regime under Law No. 9,317 (BRASIL, 1996b) and Complementary Law 123 (BRASIL, 2007).

4.3.3 Types and Basis of Calculation

a) PIS - billing (cumulative): levied on all revenue earned by the legal entity, regardless of the type of activity it carries out and the accounting classification adopted for the revenue, as determined by Law No. 9718 (BRASIL, 1998c);

b) Non-cumulative PIS: payable by legal entities that calculate income tax based on real profit. As it is non-cumulative, the company will calculate PIS on the total of its revenues, but will be able to deduct from the total due the PIS paid on purchases of goods and services acquired from legal entities, in accordance with Law 10.637 (BRASIL, 2002a);

c) PIS payroll: calculated on the value of the payroll of the following entities (BRASIL, 2001b):

- temples of any worship and political parties;
- immune educational and social assistance institutions;
- philanthropic, recreational, cultural and scientific institutions and associations exempt from income tax and CSLL;
- unions, federations and confederations;
- autonomous social services, created or authorized by law;
- supervisory boards for regulated professions;
- private law foundations and public foundations established or maintained by the public authorities;
- condominiums of residential or commercial property owners;
- Organization of Cooperatives of Brazil (OCB) and the state organizations of cooperatives.

Private Higher Education Institutions have had their revenues excluded from the non-cumulative system for calculating PIS and are subject to payment based on revenues earned (CUMULATIVE PIS). However, if they join PROUNI, they are exempt from this contribution (BRASIL. 2005a).

4.3.4 Rates

The rates applicable for determining PIS are as follows:

a) Sixty-five hundredths of a percent (0.65%): applied to the total revenue earned, including financial institutions and similar entities, as determined by Law No. 9715 (BRASIL, 1998b);

b) One whole and sixty-five hundredths percent (1.65%): applied to the non-cumulative base and determined by Law No. 10.637 (BRASIL, 2002a), and

c) One percent (1%): applied to the monthly payroll of its employees, meaning income from salaried work of any kind, such as salaries, bonuses, prizes, allowances, commissions, five-year periods, 13th salary, vacations, etc. This percentage was determined by Provisional Measure 2.158-

35 (BRASIL, 2001).

For some specific revenues, the PIS rate has been reduced to zero, such as: domestic sales of beans, rice and manioc flour, petrochemical naphtha, piped natural gas and mineral coal, domestic sales of vegetables and fruit, aircraft, their parts and other revenues.

4.3.5 PIS exemptions

Revenues and activities are exempt from PIS:

a) the export of goods abroad;

b) sales made by the producer-seller to commercial exporting companies, in accordance with Decree-Law No. 1,248 (BRAZIL, 1972);

c) sales for the specific purpose of exporting abroad;

d) the supply of goods or services for use or consumption on board ships and aircraft in international traffic, when payment is made in convertible currency;

e) from the international transportation of cargo or passengers;

f) earned by Brazilian shipyards in the construction, maintenance, modernization, conversion and repair of vessels pre-registered or registered in the Brazilian Special Registry (REB), according to Law No. 9.432 (BRASIL, 1997a);

g) freight of goods transported between the country and abroad by vessels registered with the REB;

h) arising from the sale of electricity by Itaipu Binacional, in accordance with Law No. 10.925 (BRASIL, 2004b);

i) sales to companies established in the Western Amazon, in a free trade area or in an export processing zone, in accordance with Law No. 10.833 (BRASIL, 2003), and

j) of Private Higher Education Institutions that adhere to the University for All Program - PROUNI, in accordance with Law 11.096 (BRASIL, 2005a).

These exemptions are granted by the government in order to encourage certain activities and indirectly benefit the population, as is the specific case with PROUNI.

4.4 Social Security Financing Contribution (COFINS)

The Social Security Financing Contribution (COFINS), formerly known as Finsocial, was instituted by Complementary Law No. 70 (BRASIL, 1991) and is provided for in Article 195, I of the Constitution. Its resources are earmarked exclusively to cover expenditure on related activities in the areas of health, social security and social assistance.

The total amount of the contribution collected in the country in 2006, which should be earmarked for health, was R$92,474,980,598 (ninety-two billion, four hundred and seventy-four million, nine hundred and eighty thousand, five hundred and ninety-eight reais). Of this total, the state of Ceará contributed R$ 1,151,143,969 (one billion, one hundred and fifty-one million, one hundred and forty-three thousand, nine hundred and sixty-nine reais), corresponding to a whole twenty-four percent (1.24%), according to data released by the Federal Revenue Office (SRF).

As with PIS, the Union is responsible for instituting and collecting social contributions.

The same revenues and activities that are exempt from PIS, mentioned in item 3.4.4 above, are exempt from COFINS.

4.4.1 Types and Basis of Calculation

a) COFINS - billing (cumulative): This is levied on all revenue earned by the legal entity, irrespective of the type of activity it carries out and the accounting classification adopted for the revenue, in accordance with the provisions of Law No. 9718 (BRASIL, 1998c).

b) Non-cumulative COFINS: payable by legal entities that calculate income tax based on real profit. As it is non-cumulative, the company will calculate COFINS on the total of its revenues, but will be able to deduct from the total due the COFINS paid on purchases of goods and services acquired from legal entities that earn revenues subject to the non-cumulative system, in accordance with Law No. 10.833 (BRASIL, 2003).

Private Higher Education Institutions have had their revenues excluded from the non-cumulative system for calculating COFINS and are subject to paying COFINS based on revenues earned (CUMULATIVE COFINS). However, if they join PROUNI, they are exempt from this contribution.

4.4.2 Rates

The COFINS rates are as follows:

a) three percent (3%): applied to the total revenue earned as defined in Law No. 9.718 (BRASIL , 1998c), and

b) seven whole six percent (7.6%): applied to the non-cumulative base, as set out in Law No. 10637 (BRASIL, 2002a).

The taxes mentioned in this chapter (IRPJ, CSLL, PIS and COFINS) are those directly related to PROUNI, and according to Law 11.096 (BRASIL, 2005), private higher education institutions that join the program will be exempt from them. They represent, on average, 15 % (fifteen percent) of the companies' turnover, a fact that may contribute to private higher education institutions joining the program.

5 METHODOLOGICAL PROCEDURES

Academics use scientific methodology to develop their scientific work.

scientific work. Thiollent (1983, p.55) teaches that:

> [...] it is a discipline whose objective is to analyze the characteristics of the various methods available, to evaluate their capacities, potentialities, limitations or distortions and to criticize the assumptions or implications of their use. [...] a discipline that studies the methods [...] considers as a way of conducting research.

This chapter describes the methodology used to carry out the research, following the guidance of Trivinos (1987, p. 109), who considers that at this stage "the researcher defines the research plan" and Gil (2002), who explains the case study in stages.

The methodological procedures will be detailed below, considering: the characterization of the research, its design, data collection, the study unit and the rules for data analysis and interpretation.

5.1 Characterization of the research

Based on the classification presented by Gil (2002, p.43), this research is classified as descriptive in terms of its objectives. The author states that "the main objective of descriptive research is to describe the characteristics of a given population or phenomenon".

Descriptive studies require the researcher to provide a lot of information about what he or she wishes to research and, together with exploratory studies, are usually carried out by social researchers concerned with practical action (TRIVINOS, 1987).

Trivinos (1987, p.117) classifies research, in terms of its nature, into qualitative and quantitative. In quantitative research, the variable must be "measured"; in qualitative research, the variable is "described".

Richardson (1982, p.63) states that the main difference between a qualitative and quantitative approach "lies in the fact that the qualitative approach does not employ a statistical instrument as the basis for the process of analyzing the problem".

Based on these considerations, this work is qualitative in nature, as the intention is to carry out a more dissertative analysis of the tax effects of joining PROUNI. In this specific case, the intention was not to apply statistical methods, but simply to calculate taxes based on current legislation.

According to Gil's guidelines (2002, p. 44), based on the procedures used, the research carried out is classified as bibliographical and documentary.

According to Beuren (2003, p.89): "bibliographical research makes use mainly of the contribution of various authors on a given subject of study", while documentary research "is based on materials that have not yet received an analytical treatment or that can be re-elaborated according to the objectives of the research".

To carry out the research, bibliographical surveys were carried out, consisting of doctrines and articles available on the internet.

As for documentary research, an analysis was carried out of the information recorded in the accounting statements, tax books, documents submitted to the MEC (Adhesion Agreement and Amendments), financial reports and tax legislation. This material was mainly used to analyze the tax impact of for-profit private higher education institutions as a result of joining PROUNI.

5.2 Research Design

The technical approach used in the research was a case study. According to Godoy (1995, p.25), "the case study is characterized as a type of research whose object is a unit that is analyzed in depth. It aims to examine in detail an environment, a single subject or a particular situation".

According to Gil (1999, p. 73), "the case study has been used with increasing frequency by social researchers", as it serves research with different purposes, such as: exploring real-life situations whose boundaries are not clearly defined; describing the situation of the context in which a given investigation is being carried out; and explaining causal variables of a given phenomenon in very complex situations that do not allow the use of surveys and experiments.

According to Yin (2000, p.32), the case study "allows an investigation to preserve the holistic and significant characteristics of real-life events, such as organizational and administrative processes". The aforementioned author considers the case study to be "an empirical investigation that investigates a contemporary phenomenon within its real-life context, specifically when the boundaries between the phenomenon and the context are not clearly defined" (YIN, 2002, p.20).

Following Gil's guidance (2002, 54), the case study was outlined in a set of stages listed and described below: formulation of the problem: the author defines that "the formulation of the problem is the initial stage of the research, resulting from a long process of reflection and immersion in appropriate bibliographic sources".

Definition of the case unit: according to Stake (*apud* GIL, 2002, p. 138), there are three types of case study: "intrinsic, instrumental and collective". An intrinsic case study is one in which the researcher aims to get to know the case in depth, without worrying about developing theories. Instrumental case studies, according to the author, are developed with the aim of helping to understand a particular problem. In this case, the author recognizes that it can be useful for achieving certain objectives. The author states that a "collective case study is one designed to study the characteristics of a population".

Following the above guidelines, we considered the case study to be "instrumental", as it served as a tool to help us understand the problem presented and to achieve the objectives set.

The following characteristics were taken into account when selecting the case unit: private higher education institutions based in the municipality of Fortaleza, which had joined PROUNI since it came into force (2005) and which provided data that would contribute to the development of the research.

Due to the difficulty in providing data on PROUNI at the majority of the universities selected, the research was a "single case study". However, this fact did not pose any difficulties in researching the problem and helping to achieve the objectives set, as the tax benefits offered by the federal government are common to all private institutions that join PROUNI.

Considering Yin's (2002) description, the choice of the case study as a research strategy is justified, as it allows for the detailed investigation and testing of the effects in practice of the benefits granted in the legislation that instituted PROUNI (theory).

The protocol, according to Yin (2002), includes the following sections: "project overview", with the aim of informing about the purposes for which the project was developed:

The purpose of the project, as already mentioned in previous chapters, is to evaluate the tax effect achieved by a private, for-profit Higher Education Institution located in the Municipality of Fortaleza as a result of joining the University for All Program (PROUNI). In order to achieve this, it was necessary to extend our knowledge to some subjects, such as: tax planning, current legislation on taxes related to PROUNI and the requirements for joining PROUNI.

The "field procedures" involved determining how to access the institution in order to obtain the information needed to carry out the research.

Access to the selected institution was very open, with scheduled hours, both with regard to managers and specific departments, such as accounting, the finance department, the PROUNI control department and the Technology Information Center (CTI).

5.3 Data collection

According to Gil (2002, p.55), "in terms of data collection, the case study is the most complete of all the designs, as it makes use of both people and paper data".

Yin (2002) recommends that, in a single-case study, as many sources of evidence as possible should be used. For this case study, the following sources were used: bibliographical and documentary research, personal interviews, direct and non-participatory observation.

Initially, bibliographical research was carried out in order to gather information on the characteristics of the institution being researched. The bibliographical research then focused on the concepts and procedures of tax planning, the tax burden in Brazil and worldwide and PROUNI. Books, information available on the internet and, above all, tax legislation were used.

The collection process continued with informal, personal interviews with the institution's managers, the person in charge of accounting, the PROUNI coordinator and the person in charge of the Information Technology Center (CTI), with the aim of collecting data and obtaining general information about how PROUNI worked between January 2005 and June 2006. At times, during visits to the institution, these personal interviews were carried out by technicians and assistants of the people in charge mentioned above.

For Mattar (2005, p.184), the personal interview consists of the interviewer and the interviewee(s) being in personal contact to obtain data, adding that:

The personal interview has high versatility, as it is based on personal contact. This personal contact allows the interviewer, in the event of doubts and more complex issues, to ask questions in a different way, to make clarifications and explanations not foreseen in order to elucidate them [...]. This versatility means that unstructured instruments can be applied in a personal interview without any problems.

In this study, face-to-face interviews were conducted to gather information.

In the interview with the managers, the research project was first presented and they were asked to sign a document allowing access to the institution's departments and the documentation needed to carry out the research, after which the managers reported on the history of the institution and the reasons that led them to join PROUNI.

The accounting department was asked for information on tax calculations related to PROUNI, information provided to the federal tax authorities and the release of balance sheets, income statements, tax calculation spreadsheets, financial reports, accounting and tax books containing information from January 2005 to June 2006.

The PROUNI coordinator explained all the program's operating criteria and provided PROUNI-related documentation, such as: number of students benefiting from degree courses, number of partial and total scholarships, as well as other information transmitted via SISPROUNI.

The Center for Information Technology (CTI) provided information on tuition fees, the number of students in default, the list of students benefiting from PROUNI, etc.

Exploratory research was necessary to make the research more explicit and to find out more about the effects of PROUNI, since it is a new project instituted by the current federal government. To this end, several searches were carried out on the internet and doctrines in general. However, due to the scarcity of academic work on the subject, the research was mainly limited to specific legislation.

The assessment of the tax burden of the researched institution was carried out through data analysis, i.e. it was based on the data contained in the financial statements provided by the company's accounting department and spreadsheets that supported the tax calculations.

The legislation governing the University for All Program - PROUNI was collected from the Ministry of Education's website. The legislation for each tax related to PROUNI was collected from various websites, such as: Receita Federal, Ministério da Educação, Planalto Nacional, etc.

5.4 Study Unit

The case study was carried out at a private, for-profit higher education institution located in the municipality of Fortaleza, which has been accredited with PROUNI since January 2005. In this study, the organization is referred to as "Instituiçao Construir" (fantasy name). Below are some historical aspects of this institution obtained from internal documents, the internet and interviews.

Instituiçao Construir entered the private higher education sector in 2000. However, it came from an educational group that has been working in the pre-school, primary and secondary education sector since 1935.

The Institution's mission is to build the development of society through education, providing the training of competent professionals, having been designed to meet the new demands of the knowledge society. Its teaching standard is based on an educational paradigm that has the following characteristics: competence, connection with the world of work, teaching multiple knowledge, understanding of error as part of learning, ethics and social commitment as the center, multidisciplinary vision, focus on the ability to think with autonomy, development of continuous learning, academic and interpersonal skills, consideration of the teacher as a facilitator of the teaching-learning process.

Through its own peculiarities, each course has a set of common characteristics that give the institution its own identity profile, including: a sense of mission, curricular suitability and the curriculum matrix. All the courses seek to develop intellectual skills at a higher level, enabling students to think and act in an articulate, logical and coherent way in the face of information and stimuli from the environment. The assessment of learning in each subject includes external and independent bodies, in order to guarantee quality and the achievement of high standards of performance. The results of the assessments are used to improve the system.

The institution has established a number of principles as a means of action, which are disseminated through internal documents:

a) entrepreneurial mindset and the initiative of its leaders, from strategic planning to results. Differentiation is encouraged. In return, each leader - an opportunity manager - is given authority, autonomy, resources and other appropriate means to make their units viable;

b) autonomy for educational integration in managerial, administrative and pedagogical actions. This includes recruitment activities, student and teacher selection, curriculum development, internal managerial, administrative and pedagogical integration, integration with other levels of education and supporting business activities, and liaison with the professional world and the job market;

c) efficiency to ensure the viability of the group as a whole, understood as everyone's responsibility and sought through the coordinated use of human, material and technological resources to carry out management, administrative and teaching activities. The participation of students as monitors and those responsible for school activities is part of the concept of educational and financial efficiency;

d) transparency and information - a sense of mission and the integration of activities are developed through transparent strategic and financial management mechanisms and the dissemination of up-to-date information. Each manager is responsible for ensuring that their employees have access to the necessary information.

The institution currently offers the following courses:

Level	**Course**
Undergraduate	Administration, Accounting, Law, Journalism, Pedagogy, Advertising, Information System
Postgraduate (specialization) Fortaleza	Inclusive Education, Public Accounting, Applied Linguistics, Pedagogical Coordination, Socio-educational and Therapeutic Psychodrama, Educational Informatics, Teaching of Natural Sciences and their Technologies, Law of the Financial Market, Corporate Finance, Advanced People Management, Information Security Management, Radio Broadcasting, Information Technology Business Management, Executive MBA in Auditing, Tax Planning and Management, Teaching and Literature and Reader Training, Mathematics Teaching Methodology, Communication and Culture, Software Engineering and Graphic Design. In addition to Fortaleza, the postgraduate course in Strategic Business Management is being offered in the cities of Limoeiro do Norte, Itapipoca and Sobral.
Postgraduate courses Outside Fortaleza	Strategic Business Management (Limoeiro do Norte, Itapipoca and Sobral)
Special courses	Senior citizens: art, technology, health and activities in the third sector

TABLE 9 - Courses offered by the "Construir Institution"

Source: Prepared by the author based on internal confidential documents.

Despite the various courses on offer, the institution's aim is to expand them and take them

and take them to the interior of the state, to the point of becoming a large university campus.

5.5 Data Analysis and Interpretation

All the information obtained for this study has been given a specific treatment, primarily accounting and secondarily statistical.

The values shown in Chapter 6 (six) were expressed in local currency, i.e. in Reais (R$), with cents being disregarded.

The taxes tested were calculated in accordance with the tax legislation in force, mentioned in Chapter 4 (four), i.e. PIS and COFINS were calculated on the basis of turnover, in the form of cumulative PIS and COFINS, and IRPJ and CSLL were based on real profit, calculating the operating profit in order to determine the exemption value, covering the calculation period from January 2005 to June 2006.

Through tax planning, "Instituiçao Construir" was suggested to join the University for All Program (PROUNI) as a tool capable of reducing its tax burden. The program came into effect in January 2005. From this date until June 2006, the tax effects of PROUNI were analyzed.

The tax effects on the "Construir Institution" were determined on the basis of the overall results achieved (consolidated), which were used to determine the official reduction in the tax burden levied by the federal tax authorities, and on the basis of the individual results generated by each degree course. In this second case, for internal control purposes, the study served to identify the courses that contribute most to the PROUNI tax benefit.

All the tax calculations were made using formulas structured in spreadsheets, which are explained in Chapter 6 (six).

5.6 Research boundaries

The initial intention was to carry out the research in several private higher education institutions located in the municipality of Fortaleza (multiple case study), but despite all the effort (countless visits and phone calls), the attempts were in vain, as the institutions contacted refused to make available the documents containing the data for analysis, especially the accounting documents, perhaps for fear of making the information contained therein public. The "Construir Institution", on *the other hand*, was the only one to provide all the data requested.

6 ANALYSIS OF THE TAX EFFECTS OF PROUNI ON THE CONSTRUIR INSTITUTION

Through tax planning, "Instituiçao Construir" was suggested to join PROUNI as a tool capable of reducing the tax burden. This chapter will analyze the tax effects of joining PROUNI.

In order to determine the tax effects on the "Construir Institution", it was necessary to verify the existence of tax savings achieved as a result of joining PROUNI, which were calculated in two ways:

a) on the basis of the overall results achieved (consolidated) which were used to calculate the official reduction in the tax burden levied by the federal tax authorities, and

b) based on the individual results generated by each degree course. In this case, for internal control purposes, the study served to identify the courses that contribute most to the PROUNI tax benefit.

2.1 Tax Effects Calculated Based on Overall Results (Consolidated)

The following is a calculation of the tax savings, in Reais (R$), achieved by the "Construir Institution" in the period under study, including the half-yearly tax savings as a function of the number of students benefiting from scholarships, as well as a comparison of the amounts of scholarships not received by the Institution and the tax savings achieved.

2.1.1 Fiscal savings calculated from January 2005 to June 2006

The official tax savings achieved by "Instituiçao Construir" between January 2005 and June 2006 as a result of joining PROUNI, shown in Table 6, highlights one of the objectives developed in this work (in R$), which is to determine the tax effect as a result of joining the program.

TABLE 6 - Statement of general tax savings as a result of joining PROUNI - January 2005 to June 2006, in Reais (R$)

Period	Taxes				
	PIS	COFINS	IRPJ I	CSLL	Total savings (R$)
January to June 2005	27.132	125.226	0	0	152.358
July to December 2005	28.502	131.547	0	0	160.049
January to June 2006	29.850	137.766	3.259	1.955	172.830
Tax savings	**85.484**	**394.539**	**3.259**	**1.955**	**485.237**

Source: Own elaboration.

Based on the data shown in Table 6, the tax savings generated from the start of the program (January 2005) to June 2006, amounting to R$485,237 (four hundred and eighty-five reais and two hundred and thirty-seven reais), are confirmed. The previous suggestion made through tax planning was confirmed, as there was a reduction in the tax burden of "Instituiçao Construir".

The tax savings generated each year are disclosed to the federal tax authorities for the purposes of controlling the benefit granted, through the Corporate Income Tax Return - DIPJ, which is normally submitted on the last working day of June of the following year.

A more specific analysis showed that in 2005, the tax savings came only from the PIS and COFINS taxes, which are based on turnover. In the same year, the institution calculated accounting profit, but made exclusions authorized by law from the tax calculation base (Real Profit and Social Contribution Base), which neutralized the IRPJ and CSLL calculation base (operating profit), not calculating taxes to be paid, and consequently not generating tax savings from these taxes this year.

In 2006, "Instituiçao Construir" began to calculate real profit and a positive CSLL calculation base, which led to savings in IRPJ and CSLL of R$5,214 (five thousand, two hundred and fourteen reais) in the first half of the year. It can therefore be seen that, as the institution's tax profits increase, so do its IRPJ and CSLL tax savings.

Based on the data presented in the accounting statements, it emerged that the "Construir Institution" managed to save, on average, 53% (fifty-three percent) of the total taxes due, not including labor and social security charges, in the period surveyed, as a result of having joined PROUNI. This is without taking into account IRPJ and CSLL, which are not due in 2005 because the company does not calculate operating profit (the basis for calculating these taxes).

The research was deepened in order to identify the reasons that prevented "Instituiçao Construir" from calculating tax profit, which is the basis for calculating Income Tax and Social Contribution, and identified the recording in the accounts of this institution of temporary expenses, such as the payment of installments and interest resulting from financing, which represent twenty percent (20%) of total costs and expenses. These costs and expenses reduce the profit that is the basis for calculating IRPJ and CSLL. This means that as soon as the institution finishes paying off the financing, it will make a profit capable of generating IRPJ and CSLL tax savings.

The revenue that made up the basis for calculating these taxes was that actually received, i.e. monthly arrears (defaults) were excluded from the calculation.

2.1.2 Half-Yearly Tax Savings Calculated Based on the Number of Students Benefiting from Scholarships

If we divide the total tax savings generated in each semester of the period surveyed by the number of students benefiting from PROUNI in the same period, we get the following tax benefit generated by each scholarship student:

TABLE 7 - Half-yearly statement of the tax benefit per student benefiting from PROUNI - in Reais (R$)

Period	Tax benefit in semester	Number of students benefiting	Tax benefit per student
1st semester 2005	R$152.358	80	**R$1.905**
2nd semester 2005	R$160.049	102	**R$1.569**
1st semester 2006	R$172.830	126	**R$1.372**

Source: Own elaboration.

Table 7 shows that the tax savings generated in the semester by each student benefiting from PROUNI were R$1,905 (one thousand, nine hundred and five reais) in the first semester of 2005, R$1,569 (one thousand, five hundred and sixty-nine reais) in the second semester of 2005 and R$1,372 (one thousand, three hundred and seventy-two reais) in the first semester of 2006. The value of the tax benefit achieved in each semester by each student benefiting from the program decreased over the three semesters analyzed; this was due to the tuition fee remaining almost constant, while there was an increase in the number of scholarships offered at the institution.

2.1.3 Investments with Scholarships× Tax Savings

By offering scholarships, the Construir institution did not receive the corresponding tuition fees. It remains to be seen whether the tax savings it achieves exceed or at least equal the amount it no longer receives in tuition fees. Table 8 shows the percentage of the total investment in scholarships that was recovered from the tax savings generated by joining PROUNI.

TABLE 8 - Half-yearly statement of tax savings× investments with scholarships (tuition fees not received)

Period	Tax savings (R$)	Investment in scholarships (R$)	% Recovered
1st semester 2005	152.358	173.262	**87,94**
2nd semester 2005	160.049	247.758	**64,60**
1st semester 2006	172.830	255.941	**67,53**

Source: Own elaboration.

"A Instituiçao Construir" offered 50% and 100% scholarships, totaling R$ 173,262 (one hundred and seventy-three thousand, two hundred and sixty-two reais) in the first semester of 2005, R$ 247,758 (two hundred and forty-seven thousand, seven hundred and fifty-eight reais) in the second semester of 2005, and R$ 255,941 (two hundred and fifty-five thousand, nine hundred and forty-one reais) in the first semester of 2006. Of the total amount that the Institution did not receive from scholarships in the first semester of 2005, only the equivalent of 87.94% (eighty-seven integers and ninety-four hundredths of a percent) was recovered from taxes that were no longer paid, while in the second semester 64.60% (sixty-four integers and sixty hundredths of a percent) of the amount invested was recovered, and in the first semester of 2006 67.53% (sixty-seven integers and fifty-three hundredths of a percent).

It would be feasible for the institution to at least recover the value of the scholarships entirely from the taxes that were no longer collected. In the research carried out, the institution did not achieve this desirable situation due to the lack of real profit, which is the basis for calculating income tax and social security contributions, thus causing the low recovery of these taxes. It should be noted that as the profits of "Instituiçao Construir" increase, so will the prospect of saving income tax and social security contributions.

2.2 Tax Effects Calculated on the Basis of Individual Results (By Degree Course)

What follows is a calculation of the tax savings, in reais, achieved by each "Construir Institution" undergraduate course during the period under study, the half-yearly tax savings in each undergraduate course, depending on the number of students benefiting from scholarships, as well as a comparison of the amounts of scholarships offered in each undergraduate course, not received and the tax savings achieved in each undergraduate course.

2.2.1 Fiscal savings calculated from January 2005 to June 2006

The official tax savings generated by each degree course at the "Instituiçao

Construir", in Reais (R$), in 2005 and the first semester of 2006 is as follows:

TABLE 9 - Statement of the tax savings achieved in each degree course in the period from 2005 to the first semester of 2006, in Reais (R$)

Period	Courses	Taxes				
		PIS	COFINS I	IRPJ	CSLL	Total savings (R$)
2005	Administration	17.395	80.282	21.191	35.318	**154.186**
	Pedagogy	1.598	7.377	0	0	**8.976**
	Information System	6.258	28.873	0	0	**35.129**
	Accounting	3.180	14.679	0	0	**17.859**
	Law	22.123	102.104	38.984	84.589	**247.500**
	Journalism	1.210	5.585	0	0	**6.795**
	Advertising	3.873	17.873	0	0	**21.746**
1st semester of 2006	Administration	8.053	37.166	21.609	12.099	**78.927**
	Pedagogy	901	4.160	0	0	**5.061**
	Information System	3.278	15.130	0	0	**23.469**
	Accounting Sciences	1.625	7.498	5.785	3.471	**18.379**
	Law	12.695	58.593	277.187	104.107	**452.582**
	Journalism	1.019	4.705	0	0	**5.724**
	Advertising	2.279	10.514	24.065	12.983	**49.841**

Source: Own elaboration.

Tax planning recommended joining PROUNI as a possible tool for reducing the tax burden. The data contained in table 9 confirms that all the degree courses have made tax savings as a result of the "Construir Institution" having joined PROUNI.

In 2005, the Administration and Law courses showed greater tax savings than the other courses, R$ 154,186 (one hundred and fifty-four thousand, one hundred and eighty-six reais) and R$ 247,500 (two hundred and forty-seven thousand, five hundred reais), respectively, with the same occurring in 2006. This is due to the fact that the tuition fees and the number of students are higher than those of the other courses, which consequently generate higher revenues/profits, which is the basis for calculating related taxes such as PROUNI.

Of the total number of students at "Instituiçao Construir" this year, 30% (thirty percent) are enrolled in the Administration course and 35% (thirty-five percent) in the Law course. The Law course has the highest tuition fees charged by the institution, followed by the Information Systems and

Administration courses, factors which, as mentioned above, have contributed to the tax savings of these two courses being significantly higher than the tax savings generated by the other courses.

The Law and Administration courses were the only ones to record IRPJ and CSLL tax savings in 2005, because they were the only ones to show operating profit, which is the basis for the respective taxes. The other courses only showed tax savings on the taxes levied on turnover, which are PIS and COFINS.

In the first semester of 2006, in addition to the Law and Administration courses, the Accounting and Advertising courses began to calculate profits and, consequently, tax savings on IRPJ and CSLL.

2.2.2 Tax Savings Generated in Each Undergraduate Course, Calculated in Relation to the Number of Students Benefited

The aim of calculating tax savings in relation to the number of students benefiting from PROUNI scholarships is basically to check whether the course with the highest number of students benefiting also offers the greatest tax savings, and whether the course with the lowest number of scholarship holders also has the lowest tax savings.

Table 10 shows the tax benefit achieved for each degree course, in relation to the number of students benefiting from 50% (fifty percent) and 100% (one hundred percent) scholarships, calculated over the period from January 2005 to June 2006.

TABLE 10 - Statement of the tax benefit achieved in each degree course, per student benefiting from PROUNI in the period from 2005 to the first semester of 2006, in Reais (R$)

Course	2005		1st semester 2006	
	Number of students benefiting	Tax benefit per student	Number of students benefiting	Tax benefit per student
Administration	30	**R$ 5.140**	36	**R$ 2.192**
Pedagogy	7	**R$ 1.282**	8	**R$ 633**
Information System	8	**R$ 4.391**	11	**R$ 2.134**
Accounting	5	**R$ 3.572**	7	**R$ 2.626**
Law	19	**R$ 13.026**	19	**R$ 23.820**
Journalism	4	**R$ 1.699**	8	**R$ 716**
Advertising	7	**R$ 3.107**	13	**R$ 3.834**

Source: Own elaboration.

Table 10 shows that the order of courses with the greatest tax savings in relation to the number of students benefiting from the program was as follows: Law, Administration, Advertising, Information Systems, Accounting, Journalism and Pedagogy.

Analyzing the results of table 10, it was also observed that the course with the highest number of students on grants (Administration) at the end of the second semester of 2006 is not the one with the greatest tax savings, nor is the course with the lowest number of students on grants (Accounting) the one with the lowest tax savings. This shows that the savings depend fundamentally on the amount of turnover and profits calculated, which are the basis for calculating the taxes studied, and not on the students who benefit.

As the Law course represents the one with the highest turnover, as well as the highest operating profit, it is the one that shows the greatest tax savings compared to the other courses, even if calculated in relation to the number of students benefiting from scholarships.

The Pedagogy course, on the other hand, had the lowest tax savings in relation to the number of students receiving grants, even though it is not the course with the lowest number of students benefiting from the program.

The Accounting course had the smallest number of students benefiting from the program at the end of the first semester of 2006, but it still had an average tax saving per scholarship student of R$2,066 (two thousand and sixty-six reais).

Through tax planning, the "Construir Institution" has identified the degree courses that generate the greatest tax savings. This information will help it to pay more attention (add efforts) to the courses that bring lower tax savings, in an attempt to improve its results.

2.2.3 Scholarship Investments× Tax Savings

Table 11 shows whether the tax benefit generated by each degree course exceeds or is equivalent to the total tuition fees that are not being received in full as a result of joining PROUNI.

TABLE 11 - Statement of tax savings× investments with cash (tuition fees not received) from January 2005 to June 2006, in Reais (R$)

Course	2005			1st semester 2006		
	Tax savings	Investment in scholarships	% recovered	Tax savings	Investment with cattle	% recovered
Administration	154.358	164.694	**93,72%**	78.927	87.107	**90,61%**
Pedagogy	8.976	28.980	**30,97%**	14.391	5.061	**28,44%**
Information Systems	35.129	42.042	**83,56%**	23.469	29.376	**79,89%**
Accounting	17.859	24.540	**72,78%**	18.379	11.799	**155,77%**
Law	247.500	103.992	**238%**	452.582	59.310	**763,08%**
Journalism	6.795	20.916	**32,49%**	5.724	19.044	**30,06%**
Advertising	21.746	35.856	**60,65%**	49.841	34.914	**142,75%**

Source: Own elaboration.

Table 11 shows that the only course whose tax savings excessively exceed the amount of scholarships that are no longer being received since the date of joining PROUNI (January 2005) is the Law course.

Although the Accountancy and Advertising courses did not record tax savings greater than what was being invested by the "Construir Institution" in scholarships in 2005, this situation was completely reversed in 2006, with tax savings exceeding investments in scholarships by 155.77% (one hundred and fifty-five integers and seventy-seven hundredths of a percent) and 142.75% (one hundred and forty-two integers and seventy-five hundredths), respectively.

In the Administration course, the value of the tax savings is almost as high as the value of the investment made by the "Construir Institution" with scholarships, representing a recovery of 90.61% (ninety integers and sixty-one hundredths percent) at the end of the first semester of 2006.

The Pedagogy and Journalism courses are the ones that have least recovered the value of the investment in scholarships with taxes that are no longer being paid as a result of joining PROUNI, up to the first semester of 2006. The recovery is only 28.44% (twenty-eight integers and forty-four hundredths percent) and 30.06% (thirty integers and six hundredths percent), respectively. This is because these courses have a small number of paying students, generating low turnover/profit, which is the basis for calculating PROUNI-related taxes.

This chapter aimed to analyze, using the tool of tax planning, the tax effects achieved by the "Construir Institution", in the period from January 2005 to June 2006 due to the fact that it joined PROUNI, and the conclusions about the analysis are addressed in the following chapter (conclusion).

7 Conclusion

Considering the problem, objectives and assumptions addressed, this chapter presents the final comments on the tax effects that were observed in a Private Higher Education Institution located in the Municipality of Fortaleza as a result of joining the University for All Program (PROUNI).

The dynamic environment of constant change and the search for competitive advantages makes companies seek to be more efficient in all areas of activity, and once they have reduced their taxes, they will be able to enter the market stronger. It is therefore essential to adopt an economic legal system.

In view of the Brazilian reality, it was concluded that tax planning is a useful and intelligent tool for companies to survive in an increasingly fragile and competitive market. Its adoption can contribute to the strategic growth of companies without violating the legal rules imposed by the State. When carried out responsibly by companies and with the aim of optimizing company procedures and routines, they can result in major savings in tax burdens. It is therefore an important item on the agenda for managers, capable of ensuring the optimization of their results by reducing the tax burden.

In the education sector, the weight of taxes has been the biggest obstacle to the growth of institutions. In order to avoid so many taxes, "Instituiçao Construir" chose to adopt tax planning as a fundamental tool for reducing its tax burden. By using it, they suggested joining PROUNI as a way of reducing their tax burden. Based on the data collected and analyzed from the date of joining the program (January 2005) until June 2006, the reduction in the tax burden of Instituiçao Construir was confirmed.

The results for "Instituiçao Construir" showed that it received monthly fees (invoices) throughout the period studied. As PIS and COFINS are levied on turnover, the second assumption of the research, which is that these taxes are saved, was confirmed.

The third assumption was that the tax savings on income tax and social contribution on profits were conditional on the existence of tax profits earned by private higher education institutions. The IRPJ and CSLL savings were only confirmed in the first half of 2006, when the institution began to make a tax profit.

The fourth assumption was that even though the institution had an overall (consolidated) tax loss, or low operating profit, which is the basis for calculating income tax and social security contributions, it could show a specific tax profit on some degree courses, and because of this fact and for management control purposes, it could identify the courses that would generate the greatest tax savings in income tax and social security contributions on net profit as a result of joining PROUNI. It was therefore confirmed that, in 2005, the only degree courses that generated tax profits and consequently IRPJ and CSLL savings were: Law and Administration. In the first semester of 2006, in addition to these courses, the Advertising and Accounting courses also achieved tax savings. The other courses (Pedagogy, Information System and Journalism), until the end of the first semester of 2005, had not yet contributed to IRPJ and CSLL savings. From what has been said in this paragraph, it can be concluded that all undergraduate courses generate PIS and COFINS savings, but the Law, Administration, Advertising and Accounting courses also generate IRPJ and CSLL savings, as they have shown profits, which are the basis for calculating these taxes.

The Law course had the highest number of paying students and consequently generated the highest turnover and profits, thus contributing to greater tax savings than the other courses.

The sixth assumption was that the tax savings achieved as a result of joining PROUNI should at least be equal to the investment in scholarships made by the institution, corresponding to the value of the tuition fees it did not receive. This assumption has not been confirmed, due to the fact that there is little taxable profit, which is the basis for calculating income tax and social security contributions, thus resulting in low recovery of these taxes.

Therefore, it must be considered that there are currently no vacancies on the courses offered. The "Construir Institution" is not receiving tuition fees from the beneficiary students, but it is also not incurring costs and expenses with these students, i.e. it is not opening new classrooms or hiring new teachers to serve them.

From all the above, it can be concluded that the tax effects of joining PROUNI were positively significant, since "Instituiçao Construir" stopped paying all the taxes related to PROUNI into the Union's public coffers during the period studied (PIS, COFINS, IRPJ and CSLL), representing an average tax saving of 53% (fifty-three percent) of the total taxes owed.

The University for All Program has significantly increased the number of places in higher education, internalized free education and contributed to combating social inequality.

It is hoped, therefore, that this work can offer a contribution to other private institutions wishing to join PROUNI in order to reduce their tax burden, and as a result, optimize their economic results and contribute to their continuity in the competitive market.

Further research is needed to better assess the tax effects on private higher education institutions of joining PROUNI, including comparisons with the results of other institutions. It is also suggested that the effects be analyzed not only in relation to the tuition fees that are not being received as a result of joining the program, but also in relation to costs such as teachers' and employees' salaries, electricity, costs of teaching materials, etc.

8 REFERENCES

AMARAL, Gilberto Luiz do; OLENIKE, Joao Eloi. **Brazilian tax burden** - First half of 2006. Available at: <http://www.tributarista.org.br>. Accessed on: June 20, 2006.

. **Tax burden on salaries**. Available at: <http://www.tributarista.org.br>. Accessed on: September 1, 2006.

. **The suppression of taxpayers' rights: 18 years of the 1988 Federal Constitution**. Available at:< http://www.tributarista.org.br>. Accessed on: September 1, 2006.

. **Number of regulations issued in Brazil**: 18 years of the 1988 Federal Constitution. Available at:< http://www.tributarista.org.br>. Accessed on: October 2, 2006.

. Tax Planning. In: **National Seminar on Excellence in Tax Management**. 4, 2003, Sao Paulo.

ANDRADE FILHO, Edmar Oliveira. **Normative Instruction SRF No. 456/04 and the tax regime for Private Higher Education Institutions**. Available at: <http://www.tributàrio.net/artigos/artigos_ler.asp?id=32318>. Accessed on: June 19, 2006.

AZEVEDO, Osmar Reis; SENNE, Silvio Helder Lencioni. **Tax Obligations of Non-Profit Entities and Cooperative Societies**. Sao Paulo: IOB, 2006.

BEUREN, Ilse Maria. **Como elaborar trabalhos monogrâficos em contabilidade**. Sao Paulo: Atlas, 2003.

BRAZIL. Constitution (1988). **Constitution of the Federative Republic of Brazil**. 1988a. Available at:< http://www.planalto.gov.br>. Accessed on: June 19, 2006.

. **Complementary Law No. 7**, of September 7, 1970. Establishes the Social Integration Program, and makes other provisions. 1970a. Available at: <http://www.planalto.gov.br>. Accessed on: June 19, 2006.

. **Complementary Law No. 8**, of December 3, 1970. Establishes the Public Servant Assets Formation Program, and makes other provisions. 1970b. Available at: <http://www.planalto.gov.br>. Accessed on: June 19, 2006.

. **Complementary Law no. 70**, of December 30, 1991. Institutes a contribution to finance Social Security, raises the rate of the social contribution on the profits of financial institutions and makes other provisions. 1991. Available at: <http://www.planalto.gov.br>. Accessed on: June 19, 2006.

. **Supplementary Law No. 123**, of December 14, 2006. Establishes the National Statute for Micro-enterprises and Small Businesses; amends provisions of Laws 8.212 and 8.213, both of July 24, 1991, of the Consolidation of Labor Laws - CLT, approved by Decree-Law no. 5.459, of May 1, 1943, of

Law no. 10.189, of February 14, 2001.º 5.452, de 1.° de maio de 1943, da Lei n.° 10.189, de 14 de fevereiro de 2001, da Lei Complementar n.° 63, de 11 de janeiro de 1990; e revoga as Leis n.° 9.317, de 5 de dezembro de 1996, e 9.841, de 5 de outubro de 1999. 2006a. Available at: <http://www.planalto.gov.br>. Accessed on: October 20, 2006.

. **Law No. 4.502**, of November 30, 1964. Provides for Consumption Tax and reorganizes the Internal Revenue Directorate. Available at:< http://www.fiscosoftcom.br> Accessed on: June 15, 2007.

. Law No. 5.172, of October 25, 1966. **National Tax Code**. Provides for the national tax system and establishes general tax law rules applicable to the Union, States and Municipalities. 1966. Available at:< http://www.planalto.gov.br>. Accessed on: June 20, 2006.

. Law No. 6404, of December 15, 1976. **Corporate Law**. Provides for joint stock companies. 1976. Available at:< http://www.planalto.gov.br>. Accessed on: October 20, 2006.

. **Law No. 6.435**, of July 15, 1977. Provides for private pension funds and other measures. 1977. Available at:< http://www.planalto.gov.br>. Accessed on: October 20, 2006.

. **Law No. 6.729**, of November 28, 1979. Provides for commercial concessions between producers and distributors of land motor vehicles. 1979. Available at: <http://www.planalto.gov.br>. Accessed on: October 20, 2006.

. **Law No. 7.689**, of December 15, 1988. Institutes a social contribution on the profits of legal entities, and makes other provisions. 1988b. Available at: <http://www.planalto.gov.br>. Accessed on: October 20, 2006.

. **Law No. 8.137**, of December 27, 1990. Defines crimes against the tax and economic order and against consumer relations, and makes other provisions. 1990. Available at: <http://www.fiscosoft.com.br>. Accessed on: June 15, 2007.

. **Law No. 8.981**, of January 20, 1995. Amends federal tax legislation and makes other provisions. 1995a. Available at:< http://www.planalto.gov.br>. Accessed on: October 20, 2006.

. **Law No. 9.065**, of June 20, 1995. Gives new wording to provisions of Law No. 8.981, of January 20, 1995, which amends federal tax legislation, and makes other provisions. 1995b. Available at:< http://www.planalto.gov.br>. Accessed on: October 20, 2006.

. **Law No. 9,249**, of December 26, 1995. Amends the legislation on corporate income tax and social contribution on net profit, and makes other provisions. 1995c. Available at:< http://www.planalto.gov.br>. Accessed on: October 20, 2006.

. **Law No. 9.316**, of November 22, 1996. Amends the legislation on income tax and social contribution on net profit. 1996a. Available at: <http://www.planalto.gov.br>. Accessed on: October 20, 2006.

. **Law No. 9,317**, of December 5, 1996. Provides for the tax system for micro-enterprises and small businesses, institutes the Integrated System for the Payment of Taxes and Contributions for Micro-enterprises and Small Businesses - SIMPLES and makes other provisions. 1996b. Available at:< http://www.planalto.gov.br>. Accessed on: October 20, 2006.

. Law No. 9.394, of December 20, 1996. **National Education Guidelines and Bases Law**. Establishes the guidelines and bases of national education. 1996c. Available at: <http://www.planalto.gov.br>. Accessed on: October 20, 2006.

. **Law No. 9430**, of December 27, 1996. Provides for federal tax legislation, social security contributions, the administrative consultation process and other measures. 1996d. Available at:< http://www.planalto.gov.br>. Accessed on: October 20, 2006.

. **Law No. 9.432**, of January 8, 1997. Provides for the organization of waterway transport and other measures. 1997a. Available at:< http://www.planalto.gov.br>. Accessed on: October 20, 2006.

. **Law No. 9.532**, of December 10, 1997. Amends federal tax legislation and makes other provisions. 1997b. Available at:< http://www.planalto.gov.br>. Accessed on: October 20, 2006.

. **Law No. 9710** of November 19, 1998. Provides for measures to strengthen the National Financial System and makes other provisions. 1998a. Available at: <http://www.planalto.gov.br>. Accessed on: October 20, 2006.

. **Law No. 9715**, of November 25, 1998. Provides for contributions to the Social Integration and Public Servant Assets Formation Programs - PIS/PASEP, and makes other provisions. 1998b. Available at:< http://www.planalto.gov.br>. Accessed on: October 20, 2006.

. **Law No. 9718**, of November 27, 1998. Amends Federal Tax Legislation. 1998c. Available at:< http://www.planalto.gov.br>. Accessed on: October 20, 2006.

. **Law No. 9870** of November 23, 1999. Provides for the total value of school fees and other measures. 1999a. Available at:< http://www.planalto.gov.br>. Accessed on: October 20, 2006.

. **Law No. 10.406**, of January 10, 2002. Establishes the Civil Code. Available at: <http://www.planalto.gov.br>. Accessed on: June 15, 2007.

. **Law No. 10.637**, of December 30, 2002. Provides for non-cumulative collection of contributions to the Social Integration Program (PIS) and the Public Servants' Pension Fund (PASEP), in the cases it specifies; on the payment and installment payment of federal tax debts, the offsetting of tax credits, the declaration of inaptitude to register legal entities, customs legislation, and makes other provisions. 2002a. Available at:< http://www.planalto.gov.br>. Accessed on: July 19, 2006.

. **Law No. 10.833**, of December 29, 2003. Amends Federal Tax Legislation and makes other provisions. 2003. Available at:< http://www.planalto.gov.br>. Accessed on: October 20, 2006.

. **Law No. 10.865**, of April 30, 2004. Provides for the Contribution to the Social Integration and Public Servant Assets Formation Programs and the Contribution to the Financing of Social Security levied on the import of goods and services and makes other provisions. 2004a. Available at: <http://www.planalto.gov.br>. Accessed on: October 20, 2006.

. **Law No. 10.925**, of July 23, 2004. Reduces the PIS/PASEP and COFINS rates levied on imports and domestic sales of fertilizers and pesticides and makes other provisions. 2004b. Available at: <http://www.planalto.gov.br>. Accessed on: October 20, 2006.

. **Law No. 11.033**, of December 21, 2004. Amends the taxation of the financial and capital markets; institutes the Tax Regime to Encourage the Modernization and Expansion of the Port Structure - REPORTO; amends Laws No. 10.865, of April 30, 2004, No. 8.850, of January 28, 1994, No. 8.383, of December 30, 1991, No. 10.522, of July 19, 2002, No. 9.430, of December 27, 1996, and No. 10.925, of July 23, 2004; and makes other provisions. 2004c. Available at:< http://www.planalto.gov.br>. Accessed on: October 20, 2006.

. **Law No. 11.096**, of January 13, 2005. Establishes the University for All Program - PROUNI, regulates the activities of charitable social assistance entities in higher education; amends Law No. 10.891, of July 9, 2004, and makes other provisions. 2005a. Available at: <http://www.mec.gov.br/prouni/legislaçào.br>. Accessed on: June 19, 2006.

. **Law No. 11.128**, of June 28, 2005. Provides for the University for All Program - PROUNI and amends item I of art. 2 of Law no. 11.096, of January 13, 2005. 2005b. Available at: <http://www.mec.gov.br/prouni/legislaçào.br>. Accessed on: June 19, 2006.

. **Law No. 11.196**, of November 21, 2005. Establishes the Special Taxation Regime for the Information Technology Services Export Platform - REPES, the Special Regime for the Acquisition of Capital Goods for Exporting Companies - RECAP and the Digital Inclusion Program; provides for tax incentives for technological innovation; amends Decree-Law No. 288 of February 28, 1967, Decree No. 70.235 of March 6, 1972, Decree-Law No. 2.287 of July 23, 1986, Laws No. 4.502 of November 30, 1964, No. 8.212 of July 24, 1991, No. 8.245 of October 18, 1986 and Laws No. 4.502 of November 30, 1964 and No. 8.212 of July 24, 1991.ºs 4.502, of November 30, 1964, 8.212, of July 24, 1991, 8.245, of October 18, 1991, 8.387, of December 30, 1991, 8.666, of June 21, 1993, 8.981, of January 20, 1995, 8.987, of February 13, 1995, 8.989, of February 24, 1995, 9.249, of December

26, 1995, 9.250, of December 26, 1995, 9.311, of October 24, 1996, 9.317, of December 5, 1996, 9.430, of December 27, 1996, 9.718, of November 27, 1998, 10.336, of December 19, 2001, 10.438, of April 26, 2002, 10.485, of July 3, 2002, 10.637, of December 30, 2002, 10.755, of November 3, 2003, 10.833, of December 29, 2003, 10.865, of April 30, 2004, 10.925, of July 23, 2004, 10.931, of August 2, 2004, 11.033, of December 21, 2004, 11.051, of December 29, 2004, 11.053, of December 29, 2004, 11.101, of February 9, 2005, 11.128, of June 28, 2005, and Provisional Measure 2.199-14, of August 24, 2001; repeals Law 8.661, of June 2, 1993, and provisions of Laws 8.668, of June 25, 1993, 8.981, of January 20, 1995, 10.637, of December 30, 2002, 10.755, of November 3, 2003, 10.865, of April 30, 2004, 10.931, of August 2, 2004, and Provisional Measure No. 2.158-35, of August 24, 2001; and makes other provisions. 2005c. Available at:< http://www.planalto.gov.br>. Accessed on: October 20, 2006.

. **Provisional Measure No. 2200**, of June 28, 2001. Establishes the Brazilian Public Key Infrastructure - ICP-Brasil, and makes other provisions. 2001a. Available at: <http://www.planalto.gov.br>. Accessed on: October 20, 2006.

. **Provisional Measure No. 2.158-35**, of August 24, 2001. Amends the legislation on Social Security Contributions (COFINS), Social Integration Programs (PIS/PASEP) and Income Tax, and makes other provisions. 2001b. Available at:< http://www.planalto.gov.br>. Accessed on: October 20, 2006.

. **Provisional Measure No. 213**, of September 10, 2004. Establishes the University for All Program - PROUNI, regulates the performance of charitable social assistance entities in higher education, and makes other provisions. 2004d. Available at: <http://www.planalto.gov.br>. Accessed on: October 20, 2006.

. **Decree-Law No. 1.248**, of November 29, 1972. Provides for the tax treatment of operations involving the purchase of goods on the domestic market, for the specific purpose of export, and makes other provisions. 1972. Available at:< http://www.planalto.gov.br>. Accessed on: October 20, 2006.

. **Decree No. 3000** of March 26, 1999. Regulates the taxation, inspection, collection and administration of the Tax on Income and Proceeds of Any Nature. 1999b. Available at:< http://www.planalto.gov.br>. Accessed on: June 19, 2006.

. **Decree No. 4542** of December 26, 2002. Approves the Table of Incidence of the Tax on Industrialized Products - TIPI. 2002b. Available at: <http://www.planalto.gov.br>. Accessed on: October 20, 2006.

. **Decree No. 5.493**, of July 18, 2005. Regulates the provisions of Law No. 11.096, of January 13, 2005. 2005d. Available at:< http://www.mec.gov.br>. Accessed on: June 19, 2006.

. **Decree No. 5.824**, of June 29, 2006. Establishes the procedures for granting the Qualification

Incentive and for implementing the classification by training level of civil servants who are members of the Career Plan for Technical-Administrative Positions in Education, established by Law No. 11.091, of January 12, 2005. 2006b. Available at:< http://www.planalto.gov.br>. Accessed on: October 20, 2006.

. Federal Revenue Office **Normative Instruction SRF No. 390**, of January 30, 2004. Provides for the calculation and payment of Social Contribution on Net Income. 2004b. Available at:< http://www.receita.fazenda.gov.br>. Accessed on: June 19, 2006.

. Federal Revenue Office. **SRF Normative Instruction No. 456**, of October 5, 2004. Provides for exemption from income tax and contributions applicable to institutes that adhere to the University for All Program. 2004a. Available at: <http://www.receita.fazenda.gov.br>. Accessed on: June 19, 2006.

. Minister of State for Education. **MEC Ordinance No. 4**, of May 18, 2006. Provides for the selection process of the University for All Program - PROUNI, for the second semester of 2006.2006ª. Available at:< http://www.mec.gov.br>. Accessed on: October 21, 2006.

. Minister of State for Education. **MEC Ordinance No. 1.556** of September 8, 2006. Provides for procedures for the maintenance of scholarships under the University for All Program - ProUni by higher education institutions participating in the program. 2006b. Available at: <http://www.mec.gov.br>. Accessed on: October 21, 2006.

. Minister of State for Education. **MEC Ordinance No. 1.704**, of October 18, 2006. Provides for procedures for higher education institutions to join the University for All Program - ProUni, as well as for the issuance of an Amendment to the selection process for the first semester of 2007, in the case of institutions that have already joined the program. 2006c. Available at:< http://www.mec.gov.br>. Accessed on: October 21, 2006.

. Federal Court of Auditors. National tax burden. Methodology. Lack of information on lawyers' contributions to the OAB. Considerations on the matter. Approval of the methodology and calculations. Determination to Semag. Copy forwarded. Acórdao 902/2005 - Plenàrio. Rapporteur: Benjamin Zymler. TCU, Sala das Sessoes, July 6, 2005. Available at:< http://www.tcu.gov.br>. Accessed on: August 6, 2005.

CAMPOS, Càndido H. **Planejamento tributàrio** - Imposto de Renda das Pessoas Juridicas. Sao Paulo: Atlas, 1985.

CARVALHO, Cristina Helena A. de; LOPREATO, Francisco Luiz C.. **Public Finances, Tax Revenue and ProUni in the Lula Government**. Available at: <http://www.tributàrio.net/artigos/artigos_ler.asp?id=32318>. Accessed on: June 19, 2006.

CARVALHO, Cristina Helena A.lmeida de. **Higher Education Policy and Tax Revenue**: from university reform to PROUNI. Available at:
<http://www.tributàrio.net/artigos/artigos_ler.asp?id=32318>. Accessed on: June 19, 2006.

CASSONE, Vittorio. **Tax Law**. Sao Paulo: Atlas, 1992.

FABRETTI, Làudio Camargo. **Tax accounting**. 4.ªed. Sao Paulo: Atlas: 1998.

GANDRA, Ives. **Private education suffers from high tax burden**. Available at: <http://www.fenep.org.be>. Accessed on: October 19, 2006.

GIL, Antônio Carlos. **Methods and techniques of social research**. 5th ed. Sao Paulo: Atlas, 1999.

. **Como elaborar projetos de pesquisa**. 4th ed. Sao Paulo: Atlas, 2002.

GODOY, Arilda Schmidt. Qualitative research: fundamental types**. Revista de Administraçao de Empresas**. Sao Paulo, v.35, n.3, 1995.

GONÇALVES, Hortência de Abreu. **Manual of scientific research projects**. Sao Paulo: Avercamp, 2003.

GRECO, Marco Aurélio. **Tax planning and interpretation of tax law**. Sao Paulo: Dialética, 1998.

. **Tax planning - theory and practice**. Sao Paulo: Dialética, 1998.

. **Tax planning**. Sao Paulo: Dialética, 2004.

IBC - *International Business Communications*. Available at <http://www.ibcbrasil.com.br>. Accessed on: Dec. 15, 2006.

IBGE - Brazilian Institute of Geography and Statistics. **IBGE Teen - Brazil Census - Schooling rate**. Available at <http://www.ibge.gov.br/censo/brasil500/glossario/taxa_de_escolarizaçào.htlm>. Accessed on: October 15, 2006.

IBPT - Brazilian Institute of Tax Planning. Available at <http://www.ibpt.gov.br>. Accessed on: November 20, 2006.

INEP - National Institute for Educational Studies and Research Anisio Teixeira. **Glossary of the Higher Education Census**. Available at< http://www.inep.gov.br>. Accessed on: October 15, 2006.

LATORRACA, Nilton. **Legislaçâo Tributària.** 10. ed., Sao Paulo: Atlas, 2000.

LATORRACA, Nilton. **Direito tributàrio**: imposto de renda das empresas. 15. ed. Sao Paulo: Atlas, 1999.

MACHADO, Hugo de Brito. **Tax planning** - theory and practice. Sao Paulo: Dialética, 2000.

MACULAN, Nelson; HADDAD, Fernando. Program ProUni: Changing the Panorama of Access to Higher Education in Brazil. **Revista Higher Education**, v. 12, n. 2, 2007.

MATTAR, Fauze Najib. **Marketing Research**: methodology, planning. 6th edition. Sao Paulo: Atlas, 2005.

MINISTRY OF EDUCATION.< http://www.mec.gov.br>. Accessed on: September 15, 2006.

NEVES, Silvério das. VICECONTI, Paulo E.V. **Imposto de Renda Pessoa Juridica e tributos conexos (CSLL, PIS e COFINS)**. Sao Paulo: Frase, 2004.

NEVES, Màrcio Calvet. Get to know the recent international treaties for double taxation agreements. In: **Tax planning conference** - reduce your company's tax burden according to the new regulations. Rio de Janeiro: IBC, 2005, p. 1-45.

OLIVEIRA, Airton. Panorama of Education. **Boletim do Sinepe-CE**, Fortaleza, n.37, p.2, feb., 2007.

OLIVEIRA, Luis Martins de; CHIEREGATO, Renato. **Manual de Contabilidade Tributària**. 2.ªed. Sao Paulo: Atlas, 2003.

PEIXOTO, Marcelo Magalhaes. Considerations on tax planning. In: PEIXOTO, Marcelo Magalhaes (coord.). **Planejamento tributàrio**. Sao Paulo: Quartier Latin, 2004. p. 71-87.

PEIXOTO, Marcelo Magalhaes (coord.). **Planejamento tributàrio**. Sao Paulo: Quartier Latin, 2004.

PINTO, José Marcelino de Rezende. **Access to higher education in Brazil**. 2004. Available at:< http://www.scielo.br>. Accessed on: July 12, 2006.

RECEITA FEDERAL DO BRASIL. **Carga fiscal 2005** - The tax burden and its conditioning factors. Available at: <http://www.receita.fazenda.gov.br/>. Accessed on: June 19, 2006.

. **Revenue Results** Available at: <http://www.receita.fazenda.gov.br/>. Accessed on: June 19, 2006.

RICHARDSON, Fred Nichols. **Metodologia da pesquisa em ciências sociais**: um tratamento conceptual. Sao Paulo: EPU, 1980.

ROLIM, Joao Dàcio. Tax planning as a taxpayer's right or duty - its general and specific legal contours. In: ROCHA, Valdir de Oliveira (org.). **Planejamento fiscal**: teoria e pràtica. 2. vol. Sao Paulo: Dialética: 1998. p. 49-67.

SALGADO, Kleber Bandeira. **Glossary of the Higher Education Census**. Available at: <http://www.prac.ufpb.br/antiga/censoeduc.htm>.

SILVA, André Tourinho Sancho da. **Taxes and the University for All Program (PROUNI)**. Available at: <http://www.tributàrio.net/artigos/artigos_ler.asp?id=32326>. Accessed on: June 19,

2006.

SILVA, Antônio Carlos Ribeiro da. **Metodologia da pesquisa aplicada á contabilidade**. 2.ªed. Sao Paulo: Atlas: 2006.

SOUSA, Rubens Gomes de. **Compêndio de legislaçao tributària**. ed. póst. Sao Paulo: Resenha Tributària, 1975.

. **PROUNI tax benefits**. Available at: <http://www.tributàrio.net/artigos/artigos_ler.asp?id=32418>. Accessed on: June 19, 2006.

THIOLLENT, Michel. Problems of methodology. In: FLEURY, Afonso Carlos Correa & VARGAS, Nilton (orgs). **Organizaçao do trabalho**. Sao Paulo, Atlas, 1983.

TÔRRES, Heleno. **International tax law: tax planning and transnational operations**. Sao Paulo: Revista dos Tribunais, 2001.

TRIVINOS, Augusto N. S. **Introduçao à pesquisa** em **ciências sociais** - A pesquisa qualitativa em educaçao. Sao Paulo: Atlas, 1987.

FEDERAL UNIVERSITY OF CEARA. Science and Technology Library. **Guide to standardizing academic work according to the Brazilian Association of Technical Standards (ABNT)**. Fortaleza, 2003. 76 p.

YIN, Roberto K. **Case study**: planning and methods. 2. ed. Porto Alegre: Bookman, 2002.

ANNEX

ANNEX A - LAW NO. 11.096, OF JANUARY 13, 2005

Establishes the University for All Program - PROUNI, regulates the activities of charitable social assistance entities in higher education; amends Law No. 10.891, of July 9, 2004, and makes other provisions.

THE PRESIDENT OF THE REPUBLIC I hereby inform you that the National Congress has decreed and I hereby sanction the following Law:

Art. 1. The University for All Program - PROUNI - is hereby instituted, under the management of the Ministry of Education, for the granting of full scholarships and partial scholarships of 50% (fifty percent) or 25% (twenty-five percent) for students in undergraduate and sequential courses of specific training, in private higher education institutions, whether for-profit or not.

§ 1 ° Full scholarships will be awarded to Brazilians who do not have a university degree and whose monthly per capita family income does not exceed one and a half (1/2) times the minimum wage.

§ 2 ° Partial scholarships of 50% (fifty percent) or 25% (twenty-five percent), the distribution criteria for which will be defined in regulations by the Ministry of Education, will be granted to Brazilians who do not hold a higher education degree, whose monthly family income per capita does not exceed the value of up to 3 (three) minimum wages, according to criteria defined by the Ministry of Education.

§ 3 For the purposes of this Law, a scholarship refers to the semester or annual tuition fees established on the basis of Law No. 9,870 of November 23, 1999.

§ Paragraph *4.* For the purposes of this Law, partial study grants of 50% (fifty percent) or 25% (twenty-five percent) shall be awarded, taking into account all regular and collective discounts offered by the institution, including those given as a result of punctual payment of tuition fees.

Art. 2: The scholarship will be intended for:

I - to students who have completed their secondary education in public schools or private institutions as full scholarship students;

II - disabled students, under the terms of the law;

III - a teacher from the public school system, for degree courses, higher normal education and pedagogy, aimed at training teachers in basic education, regardless of the income referred to in §§ 1 and 2 of art. 1 of this Law.

Sole paragraph. The maintenance of the scholarship by the beneficiary, observing the maximum deadline for completion of the degree course or specific training sequence, will depend on the fulfillment of academic performance requirements, established in norms issued by the Ministry of Education.

Art. 3 The student to benefit from Prouni will be pre-selected based on the results and socio-economic profile of the National High School Exam - ENEM or other criteria to be defined by the Ministry of Education and, in the final stage, selected by the higher education institution, according to its own criteria, which will also be responsible for assessing the information provided by the candidate.

Sole paragraph. Prouni beneficiaries are legally responsible for the veracity and authenticity of the socio-economic information they provide.

Art. 4 All the institution's students, including Prouni beneficiaries, will also be governed by the same internal rules and regulations.

Art. 5.Private higher education institutions, whether for-profit or not-for-profit, may join Prouni by signing an agreement, and must offer a minimum of 1 (one) full scholarship for the equivalent of 10,7 (ten integers and seven tenths) regularly paying students duly enrolled at the end of the corresponding previous academic period, in accordance with the regulations to be established by the Ministry of Education, excluding the number corresponding to full scholarships granted by Prouni or by the institution itself, in courses actually held at the institution.

§ 1 The term of the agreement will be 10 (ten) years, counting from the date it is signed, renewable for equal periods and subject to the provisions of this Law.

§ 2 The agreement may provide for the exchange of scholarships between courses and shifts, restricted to 1/5 (one fifth) of the scholarships offered for each course and each shift.

§ 3 ° The termination of the adhesion agreement, at the initiative of the private institution, will not entail any burden for the Public Power or any loss for the student benefiting from Prouni, who will enjoy the benefit granted until the completion of the course, respecting the internal rules of the institution, including disciplinary rules, and observing the provisions of art. 4 of this Law.

§ 4 The private for-profit or non-profit non-benefit higher education institution may, alternatively, as a substitute for the requirement laid down in the *caput of* this article, offer 1 (one) full scholarship for every 22 (twenty-two) regularly paying students and duly enrolled in courses actually held there, in accordance with regulations to be established by the Ministry of Education, provided that it additionally offers a number of partial scholarships of 50% (fifty percent) or 25% (twenty-five percent) in the proportion necessary for the sum of the benefits granted under this Law to reach the equivalent of 8.5% (eight integers and five tenths percent) of the annual revenue of the school periods that already have Prouni scholarship holders, effectively received under the terms of Law no.° 9.870, of November 23, 1999, in undergraduate or sequential courses of specific training.

§ 5 ° For 2005, private higher education institutions, whether for profit or nonprofit, may:

I - adhere to Prouni by signing an adhesion agreement, whereby it must offer at least 1 (one) full scholarship for every 9 (nine) students regularly paying and duly enrolled at the end of the corresponding previous academic period, in accordance with regulations to be established by the Ministry of Education, excluding the number corresponding to full scholarships granted by Prouni or by the institution itself, in courses actually held there;

II - alternatively, as a substitute for the requirement set out in item I of this paragraph, offer 1 (one) full scholarship for every 19 (nineteen) regularly paying students duly enrolled in courses actually offered by the institution, in accordance with regulations to be established by the Ministry of Education, provided that it additionally offers, a number of partial scholarships of 50% (fifty percent) or 25% (twenty-five percent) in the proportion necessary for the sum of the benefits granted under this Law to reach the equivalent of 10% (ten percent) of the annual revenue of the school periods that already have Prouni scholarship holders, effectively received under the terms of Law no. 9.870, of 23 July.° 9.870, de 23 de novembro de 1999, in undergraduate or sequential courses of specific training.

§ 6 ° The provisions of § 5 of this article shall apply to the initial classes of each course and shift actually installed as of the 1st (first) selection process following the publication of this Law, until the proportions established for all students of the institution's undergraduate and sequential courses of specific training are reached, and the provisions of the *caput* and § 4 of this article shall apply to the initial classes *of* each course and shift actually installed as *of* the 1st (first) selection process following the publication of this Law, until *the* proportions established for all students of the institution's undergraduate and sequential courses of specific training are reached.The provisions of the caput and § 4 of this article shall apply to the initial classes of each course and shift actually installed as from the 2006 financial year, until the proportions established for all students on the institution's specific undergraduate and sequential courses are reached.

Art. 6 As soon as the proportion established in §6 of art. 5 of this Law is reached for all the students on the institution's undergraduate and sequential courses of specific training, whenever the drop-out rate of the students benefited shows a discrepancy in relation to the drop-out rate of the other students enrolled, the institution will, at each selection process, offer scholarships in the proportion necessary to establish that proportion.

Art. 7 The obligations to be fulfilled by the higher education institution will be set out in the Prouni agreement, which must include the following necessary clauses:

I - the proportion of scholarships offered per course, shift and unit, respecting the parameters established in Article 5 of this Law;

II - the percentage of scholarships earmarked for the implementation of affirmative policies for access to higher education for people with disabilities or self-declared indigenous and black people.

§ 1 ° The percentage referred to in item II of the *caput of* this article must be at least equal to the percentage of self-declared indigenous, brown or black citizens in the respective unit of the Federation, according to the last census of the Brazilian Institute of Geography and Statistics - IBGE.

§ 2 ° If the vacancies are not filled according to the criteria in § 1 of this article, the remaining vacancies must be filled by students who meet one of the criteria in articles 1 and 2 of this Law.

§ 3 ° Higher education institutions that do not enjoy autonomy are authorized to increase the number of places on their courses, as soon as the agreement is signed, within the limits of the proportion of full scholarships offered per course and shift, in accordance with the regulations.

§ 4 The Ministry of Education will withdraw from Prouni a course deemed insufficient, without prejudice to the student already enrolled, according to the performance criteria of the National Higher Education Evaluation System - SINAES, for 3 (three) consecutive evaluations, in which case the scholarships for the withdrawn course, in the following selection processes, will have to be redistributed proportionally among the other courses of the institution, respecting the provisions of art. 5 of this Law.

§ 5 ° Students on the courses referred to in paragraph 4 of this article will be allowed to transfer to an identical or equivalent course offered by another institution participating in the Program, with priority being given to Prouni scholarship holders.

Art. 8: The institution that joins Prouni will be exempt from the following taxes and contributions during the term of the agreement: (See Provisional Measure No. 235 of 2005)

I - Corporate Income Tax;

II - Social Contribution on Net Profit, instituted by Law No. 7.689, of December 15, 1988;

III - Social Contribution for the Financing of Social Security, instituted by Complementary Law No. 70, of December 30, 1991; and

IV - Contribution to the Social Integration Program, instituted by Complementary Law No. 7, of September 7, 1970.

§ 1 ° The exemption referred to in the *caput of* this article will apply to profit in the cases of items I and II of the *caput of* this article, and to revenue earned in the cases of items III and IV of the *caput of* this article, arising from the performance of higher education activities, from undergraduate courses or sequential courses of specific training.

§ 2 ° The Federal Revenue Office of the Ministry of Finance will regulate the provisions of this article within 30 (thirty) days.

Art. 9 Failure to comply with the obligations assumed in the adhesion agreement shall subject the institution to the following penalties:

I - re-establishment of the number of scholarships to be offered free of charge, which will be determined at each selection process, whenever the institution fails to comply with the percentage established in Art. 5 of this Law and which must be sufficient to maintain the percentage established therein, with an increase of 1/5 (one fifth);

II - disconnection from Prouni, determined in the event of recidivism, in the event of serious misconduct, as provided for in the regulations, without prejudice to the students benefiting and without cost to the Public Authorities.

§ 1 The penalties provided for in the *caput of* this article will be applied by the Ministry of Education, under the terms of the regulations, after an administrative procedure has been initiated, with the right to an adversarial hearing and the right to a defense assured.

§ 2 In the event of item II of the *caput* of this article, the suspension of the exemption from the taxes and contributions referred to in Article 8 of this Law shall have as its initial term the date of occurrence of the fault which caused the disconnection from Prouni, and the provisions of Articles 32 and 44 of Law No. 9430, of December 27, 1996, shall apply where applicable.

§ 3 The penalties provided for in the *caput of* this article may not be applied when the failure to comply with the obligations assumed is due to reasons to which the institution did not give rise.

Art. 10: Higher education institutions, even if they are active in basic education or in areas other than education, can only be considered charitable social assistance organizations if they offer at least one full scholarship to a student on a degree course or specific training course, without a degree, who falls under §1 of art. 1 of this law.Paragraph 1 of Article 1 of this Law, for every 9 (nine) paying students of the institution's regular undergraduate or sequential courses of specific training, enrolled in courses that have actually been installed, and meet the other legal requirements.

§ 4 ° The institution referred to in the *caput of* this article must apply at least 20% (twenty percent) of its gross revenue from the sale of services, plus revenue from financial investments, the rental of goods, the sale of goods that are not part of fixed assets and private donations, to free services every year, respecting, where applicable, the rules governing the activities of charitable social assistance entities in the health sector.

§ 5 ° In order to comply with the provisions of § 1 of this article, in addition to the full scholarships referred to in *the caput of* this article, partial scholarships of 50% (fifty percent) or 25% (twenty-five percent) for students falling under § 2 of art. 1 of this Law and social assistance in programs not arising from curricular teaching and research obligations shall be accounted for.

§ 6 The provisions of the *caput of* this article shall apply to the initial classes of each course and shift actually installed as of the 1st (first) selection process following the publication of this Law.

§ 7 ° As soon as the proportion established in the *caput of* this article is reached for all students on the institution's undergraduate and sequential specific training courses, whenever the dropout rate of the students benefiting from the scholarship shows a discrepancy in relation to the dropout rate of the other enrolled students, the institution will offer full scholarships at each selection process in the proportion necessary to re-establish that proportion.

§ 8 Scholarships may be exchanged between courses and shifts, limited to 1/5 (one fifth) of the scholarships offered for each course and each shift.

Art. 11 - Charitable social assistance entities operating in higher education may, by signing an agreement with the Ministry of Education, adopt the Prouni rules contained in this Law for selecting students benefiting from full scholarships and partial scholarships of 50% (fifty percent) or 25% (twenty-five percent), in particular the rules set out in art. 3 and in subsection 3 of this Law. 3 and in item II of the *heading* and §§ 1 and 2 of Article 7 of this Law, undertaking, for the term of the agreement, limited to 10 (ten) years, renewable for equal periods, and respecting the provisions of Article 10 of this Law, to comply with the following conditions:

I - offer 20% (twenty percent), free of charge, of their annual revenue actually received under the terms of Law 9.870, of November 23, 1999, being exempt from complying with the requirement of § 1 of art. 10 of this Law, provided that the rules governing the performance of charitable social assistance entities in the health area are respected, where applicable;

II - in order to comply with the provisions of item I of the *caput of* this article, the institution:

a) must offer at least 1 (one) full scholarship to a student in a specific undergraduate or graduate course, without a higher education diploma, falling within the scope of § 1 of art. 1 of this Law, for every 9 (nine) paying students in a specific undergraduate or graduate course of the institution, enrolled in courses effectively installed, subject to the provisions of §§ 3, 4 and 5 of art. 10 of this Law;

b) may account for the amounts spent on full and partial scholarships of 50% (fifty percent) or 25% (twenty-five percent), intended for students falling under § 2 of Art. 1 of this Law, and the amount directed to social assistance in programs not arising from curricular teaching and research obligations;

III - enjoy the benefit provided for in Paragraph 3 of Article 7 of this Law.

§ 1 The Ministry of Education is responsible for verifying and informing the other bodies concerned of the entity's situation in relation to compliance with Prouni's requirements, without prejudice to the powers of the Federal Revenue Office and the Ministry of Social Security.

§ 2 Charitable social assistance entities that have had their applications for renewal of the Certificate of Charitable Social Assistance Entity rejected in the last two (2) three-year periods, solely because they did not meet the minimum percentage of gratuity required, which adopt the Prouni rules, under the terms of this Law, may, up to 60 (sixty) days after the date of publication of this Law, apply to the National Social Assistance Council (CNAS) for a new Certificate of Beneficent Social Assistance Entity and, subsequently, apply to the Ministry of Social Security for exemption from the contributions referred to in art. 55 of Law No. 8212 of July 24, 1991.

§ 3 The Ministry of Social Security will decide on the exemption request of the entity that obtains the Certificate in the form of the *caput of* this article with effect from the issuance of Provisional Measure No. 213, of September 10, 2004, and it will be up to the entity to prove to the Ministry of Social Security the effective fulfillment of the obligations assumed, until the last day of the month of April following each of the next 3 (three) fiscal years.

§ 4 In the event that the CNAS does not decide on the request by March 31, 2005, the entity may submit a request for exemption to the Ministry of Social Security, regardless of the CNAS's decision, by presenting a copy of the request sent to the CNAS and the respective protocol of receipt.

§ 5 The provisions of Article 55 of Law No. 8212 of July 24, 1991 shall apply to the exemption request referred to in this article.

Art. 12 - Once the socio-economic conditions set out in §§1 and 2 of art. 1 of this Law have been met, the institutions that join Prouni or adopt its selection rules may consider workers from the institution itself and their dependents who are scholarship recipients as a result of a collective bargaining agreement or labor agreement as scholarship recipients of the program, up to a limit of 10% (ten percent) of the Prouni scholarships awarded.

Art. 13: Legal entities governed by private law, which maintain non-profit higher education institutions, which adopt the rules for selecting scholarship students referred to in art. 11 of this Law and which are exempt from the social security contribution referred to in § 7 of art. 195 of the Federal Constitution, who opt, as of the date of publication of this Law, to transform their legal nature into an economic purposes company, in the manner permitted by art. 7-A of Law no. 9.131, of November 24, 1995, will pay the employer's social security contribution gradually, over a period of 5 (five) years, at the rate of 20% (twenty percent) of the amount due each year, cumulatively, until reaching the full amount of the contributions due.

Sole Paragraph. The private law legal entity transformed into an economic purposes company will start paying the social security contribution referred to in the *caput of* this article as of the 1st day of the month in which the general meeting authorizing the transformation of its legal nature is held, respecting the grade corresponding to the respective year.

Art. 14. Priority in the distribution of resources available in the Higher Education Student Financing Fund (FIES) shall be given to private law institutions that adhere to Prouni in accordance with art. 5 of this Law or adopt the rules for selecting scholarship students referred to in art. 11 of this Law.

Art. 15. For the purposes of this Law, the provisions of art. 6 of Law no. 10.522, of July 19, 2002, will be required from 2006 onwards of all higher education institutions adhering to Prouni, including the validity of Provisional Measure no. 213, of September 10, 2004.

Art. 16. The process for the Ministry of Education to approve the term of adhesion, under the terms of art. 5 of this Law, shall be instructed with the estimate of the tax waiver, in the year of approval and in the two (2) subsequent years, to be enjoyed by the respective institution, under the terms of art. 9 of this Law, as well as the estimate of the tax waiver, in the year of approval and in the two (2) subsequent years, to be enjoyed by the respective institution, under the terms of art. 9 of this Law. 9 of this Law, as well as a statement of the compensation for this tax break, the growth in the collection of federal taxes and contributions in the same economic segment or the previous reduction in ongoing expenses.

Sole paragraph. The evolution of tax collection and tax waivers for private higher education institutions will be monitored by an inter-ministerial group, made up of 1 (one) representative from the Ministry of Education, 1 (one) from the Ministry of Finance and 1 (one) from the Ministry of Social Security, which will provide the necessary subsidies for the implementation of the provisions in the *caput of* this article.

Art. 17 (VETOED).

Art. 18 - The Executive Branch shall publicize the results of the Program on an annual basis.

Art. 19. The terms of adhesion signed during the term of Provisional Measure No. 213, of September 10, 2004, shall be valid for the period specified therein, subject to the provisions of § 4 and *caput of* art. 5 of this Law.

Art. 20 The Executive Branch shall regulate the provisions of this Law.

Article 21 - Items I, II and VII of the *caput of* Article 3 of Law No. 10.891, of July 9, 2004, shall come into force with the following wording:

"Art. 3..

I - be at least 14 (fourteen) years old to obtain the National Athlete, International Olympic and Paralympic Athlete Grants, and be at least 12 (twelve) years old to obtain the Student Athlete Grant;

II - be linked to a sports organization, except for athletes applying for the Student Athlete Grant;

VII - be regularly enrolled in a public or private educational institution, exclusively for athletes who apply for the Student Athlete Grant." (NR)

Art. 22 Annex I of Law No. 10.891, of July 9, 2004, shall come into force with the alteration set out in Annex I of this Law.

Art. 23 This Law shall enter into force on the date of its publication.

Brasilia, January 13, 2005; 184th of Independence and 117th of the Republic.

LUIZ INACIO LULA DA SILVA. Antonio Palocci Filho Tarso Genro.

ANNEX B - DECREE NO. 5.493, OF JULY 18, 2005

Regulates the provisions of Law No. 11.096, of January 13, 2005.

THE PRESIDENT OF THE REPUBLIC, using the powers conferred on him by Article 84, IV of the Constitution, and in view of the provisions of Law No. 11.096, of January 13, 2005,

DECREES:

Art. 1 The University for All Program - PROUNI, referred to in Law No. 11.096, of January 13, 2005, is aimed at granting full scholarships and partial scholarships of fifty percent or twenty-five percent, for students in undergraduate or sequential courses of specific training, in private institutions of higher education, whether for-profit or not-for-profit, which have adhered to PROUNI under the terms of the applicable legislation and the provisions of this Decree.

Sole paragraph. For the purposes of enjoying tax benefits, the term of adhesion may not cover courses that require prior higher education training as a requirement for enrollment.

Art. 2: PROUNI will be implemented through the Higher Education Secretariat of the Ministry of Education.

§ 6 ° Higher education institutions interested in joining PROUNI will sign an agreement with the Ministry of Education.

§ 7 ° Scholarships may be canceled at any time if a document presented or information provided by the scholarship holder is found to be inaccurate.

§ 8 The accumulation of scholarships linked to PROUNI is prohibited, as is the granting of a scholarship linked to it to a student enrolled in a free public higher education institution.

§ 9 The Ministry of Education will decide on the operational procedures for joining PROUNI and selecting scholarship holders, especially as regards the definition of the cut-off point and the methods for filling any remaining vacancies, including those arising from the legal percentage earmarked for affirmative policies for access by people with disabilities or self-declared black and indigenous people.

Art. 3: The teacher benefiting from a full or partial scholarship linked to PROUNI must be working as a teacher in basic education, as part of the permanent staff of a public institution.

Art. 4: The pre-selection of students to benefit from PROUNI will be based on the result obtained in the National High School Exam - ENEM for the edition immediately preceding the PROUNI selection process for admission to a degree course or specific training sequence.

Art. 5 For the purposes of calculating the number of scholarships to be offered by the institutions that adhere to PROUNI or by charitable social assistance entities that operate in higher education, regularly paying students are those who have signed an onerous contract with a higher education institution based on Law no. 9.870, of 23 July.º 9.870, de 23 de novembro de 1999, who are not beneficiaries of full scholarships from PROUNI or from the institution itself, excluding those in default for a period of more than ninety days, whose enrollments have been refused in the academic period immediately following the default, under the terms of arts. 5 and 6 of that Law.

Sole paragraph. For the purposes of calculating the number of full scholarships to be granted by educational institutions, beneficiaries of partial scholarships of fifty percent or twenty-five percent are considered to be regular paying students, without prejudice to the provisions of the caput.

Art. 6 Higher education institutions that adhere to PROUNI under the terms of the rule provided for in § 4 of art. 5 of Law no. 11.096, of 2005, may offer full scholarships in an amount greater than the legal minimum, provided that the total of full and partial scholarships makes up a proportion equivalent to eight and five-tenths percent of the annual revenue of the academic periods that already have PROUNI scholars, effectively received under the terms of Law no. 9.870, of 1999.

Art. 7 Higher education institutions, whether for-profit or not, including social assistance charities, may convert up to ten percent of the partial scholarships of fifty percent linked to PROUNI into partial scholarships of twenty-five percent, at the rate of two partial scholarships of twenty-five percent for each partial scholarship of fifty percent, in undergraduate or sequential courses of specific training, whose portion of the annual fee or semester fee actually charged, based on Law no. 9.870, 1999.º 9.870, de 1999, does not exceed, individually, the value of R$ 200,00 (two hundred reais).

Art. 8 Higher education institutions, whether for profit or not, including social assistance charities, may offer full and partial scholarships of fifty percent in addition to those provided for in their respective terms of adhesion, aimed exclusively at new students.

Sole paragraph. The scholarships referred to in the *caput* will be counted as PROUNI scholarships and may be compensated for in subsequent academic periods, at the discretion of the higher education institution, provided that the minimum proportion legally required, by course and shift, is met in the academic periods that already have PROUNI scholarship holders.

Art. 9 The sum of the benefits granted by the higher education institution will be calculated considering the arithmetic average of the annual or semester fees actually charged to regularly paying students, under the terms of this Decree, excluding students benefiting from partial scholarships, including those benefiting from the additional scholarships referred to in art. 8.

Art. 10 - The exchange of scholarships between courses and shifts, when provided for in the agreement, is restricted to one fifth of the scholarships offered for each course and shift, and the number of scholarships resulting from the exchange may not be higher or lower than this limit for each course or shift.

Art. 11: Higher education institutions that do not enjoy autonomy are authorized, as of the signing of the PROUNI agreement, to increase the number of places on their courses, subject to the following conditions:

I - in strict compliance with the number of full scholarships actually offered by the higher education institution, after possible exchanges of scholarships between courses and shifts, observing the relevant rules; and

II - exceptionally, to restore the ratio between full and partial scholarships originally set out in the agreement, solely and exclusively to compensate for school drop-outs by students with full or partial scholarships linked to PROUNI.

Art. 12 - If there are indications of non-compliance with the obligations assumed in the agreement, an administrative procedure will be set up to assess the responsibility of the higher education institution involved, applying the penalties provided for, if applicable.

§ 1 ° The provisions of Law No. 9.784, of January 29, 1999, shall apply to the administrative procedure provided for in the *caput*, where applicable, observing the adversarial process and a full defense.

§ 2 For the purposes of this Decree, serious misconduct is considered to be

I - repeated non-compliance with the infraction provided for in item I of Article 9 of Law No.

11,096 of 2005, ascertained in a prior administrative proceeding;

II - instituting discriminatory treatment between paying students and PROUNI beneficiaries;

III - misrepresent the information provided in the application form, in order to unduly reduce the number of full and partial scholarships to be offered; and

IV - misrepresenting the information provided in the application form in order to unduly expand the scope of the tax benefits provided for in PROUNI.

§ 3 ° The decision to impose a penalty may be appealed to the Minister of State for Education.

Art. 13 - For the calculation of the application in gratuity referred to in art. 10 of Law 11.096, of 2005, full scholarships, partial scholarships of fifty percent or twenty-five percent and social assistance in programs not resulting from curricular teaching and research obligations will be counted, when referring to the initial classes of each course and shift actually installed as of the first selection process after the publication of the aforementioned Law.

Sole paragraph. For the calculation provided for in the *caput*, regarding classes started before September 13, 2004, the benefits granted to students under the terms of the applicable legislation may be taken into account.

Art. 14: The higher education institution that joins PROUNI will submit to the Ministry of Education, every semester, in accordance with the respective academic curriculum:

I - control of the minimum compulsory attendance of the scholarship holders, corresponding to seventy-five percent of the course load;

II - the performance of the scholarship holders on the course, taking into account, in particular, their academic performance ; and

III - the dropout rate of students by course and shift, as well as the total number of students enrolled, listing the students linked to PROUNI.

§ 1 The charitable social assistance entity that operates in higher education and adheres to PROUNI will send the Ministry of Education a report on its activities and spending on social assistance no later than sixty days after the end of the fiscal year.

§ 2 ° The development of social assistance programs in accordance with the provisions of Law No. 8.742, of December 7, 1993, which are not part of the compulsory curriculum of undergraduate and sequential courses of specific training, is considered social assistance in programs not arising from curricular obligations of teaching and research.

§ 3 The Ministry of Education will establish the academic performance requirements to be met by the student linked to PROUNI, for the purposes of maintaining the scholarships.

Art. 15 - The scholarships reserved for employees of the higher education institution and their dependents as a result of a collective bargaining agreement or labor agreement, under the terms of the law, will be filled in compliance with the operational procedures established by the Ministry of Education, especially as regards the definition of the cut-off score for the selection of scholarship holders and the methods for taking advantage of any remaining vacancies, without prejudice to pre-selection, according to the results of the ENEM.

Sole paragraph. The higher education institution interested in granting scholarships linked to PROUNI, under the terms of the *caput*, must previously inform the Ministry of Education and send a certified copy of the legal acts that formalize the collective bargaining agreement or labor agreement, with the respective subsequent amendments.

Art. 16: The sponsors of higher education institutions that choose to transform their legal nature into an economic purposes company, under the terms of art. 7-A of Law 9.131, of November 24, 1995, must ensure the continuity of the scholarships granted to the classes started before September 13, 2004, for the five years foreseen for the transformation of the legal regime.

Art. 17: The monitoring and social control of the procedures for awarding scholarships under PROUNI will be carried out:

I - by a national committee, with a predominantly advisory role on national implementation guidelines;

II - by local monitoring committees, whose main function is to monitor, investigate and supervise local implementation.

Sole paragraph. The Ministry of Education will define the duties and criteria for the composition of the national committee and the monitoring committees.

Art. 18 This Decree comes into force on the date of its publication.

Art. 19 Decree No. 5.245 of October 15, 2004 is hereby revoked.

Brasilia, July 18, 2005; 184th of Independence and 117th of the Republic.

LUIZ INACIO LULA DA SILVA

Tarso Genro

ANNEX C - SRF NORMATIVE INSTRUCTION NO. 456, OF OCTOBER 5, 2004

(DOU 08.10.2004)

Provides for the exemption from income tax and contributions applicable to institutions that join the

University for All Program.

The Secretary of the Federal Revenue Service, using the powers conferred on him by item III of art. 209 of the Internal Regulations of the Federal Revenue Service, approved by MF Ordinance no. 259, of August 24, 2001, and in view of the provisions of Provisional Measure no. 213, of September 10, 2004, resolves:

Art. 1: The private higher education institution, for-profit or non-benefit, which adheres to the University for All Program (Prouni) under the terms of art. 5 of Provisional Measure No. 213, of 2004, will be exempt, during the period of validity of the adhesion term, from the following contributions and taxes:

I - Social Security Financing Contribution (Cofins);

II - Contribution to PIS/Pasep;

III - Social Contribution on Net Profits (CSLL); and

IV - Corporate Income Tax (IRPJ).

§ 1 ° The exemption referred to in the *caput* shall apply to profit in the case of items III and IV, and to the amount of revenue earned in the case of items I and II, arising from the performance of higher education activities, from undergraduate courses or sequential courses of specific training.

§ 2 ° For the purposes of the provisions of items III and IV of the *caput*, the educational institution must calculate the operating profit relating to the activities on which the exemption falls, in compliance with the provisions of art. 2 and the income tax legislation.

Art. 2. The operating profit referred to in §2 of art. 1 shall be deemed to be the net profit for the calculation period, before deduction of the provision for CSLL and the provision for income tax, adjusted by the exclusion of the following amounts:

I - the part of financial income that exceeds financial expenses;

II - income and losses from shareholdings;

III - non-operating results; and

IV - the amount written off the revaluation reserve, in cases where the realized value of the assets subject to revaluation has been recorded as an operating cost or expense and the write-off of the reserve has been made against the account of:

a) non-operating income; or

b) net equity, not computed in the result for the same period.

Sole paragraph. Monetary variations will be considered, for the purposes of calculating operating profit, as financial income or expenses, as the case may be.

Art. 3 - In order to benefit from the exemption, the educational institution must clearly and accurately demonstrate in its accounts the elements that make up the income, costs, expenses and results for the assessment period, relating to the activities on which the exemption falls, segregated from other activities.

Sole paragraph. In the event that the accounting system adopted by the educational institution does not offer conditions for calculating net profit and operating profit by activity, this may be established on the basis of the ratio between net revenue from exempt activities and total net revenue.

Art. 4 The commission of acts that constitute crimes against the tax order, as well as the failure to issue invoices, will result in the offending legal entity losing, in the corresponding calendar year, the benefit of the exemption referred to in art. 1.

Sole Paragraph. The granting or recognition of any tax incentive or benefit relating to the contributions and taxes referred to in Article 1 shall be conditional on the taxpayer proving that they have been duly paid.

Art. 5: If the institution is disconnected from Prouni, the exemption from the contributions and tax referred to in art. 1 will be suspended from the date of occurrence of the fault giving rise to the suspension, covering the entire period of assessment of the tax or contributions.

§ 1 ° When it is found that the institution benefiting from the exemption is not complying with the requirements or conditions pertinent to the matter or provided for in tax legislation, the tax inspectorate will issue a tax notification, in which it will report the facts that determine the suspension of the benefit, including the date on which the infraction occurred.

§ 2 ° The institution may, within thirty days of receiving the notification, present the allegations and evidence it deems necessary.

§ 3 The Federal Revenue Delegate will decide whether the allegations are well-founded, issuing a declaratory act suspending the exemption if they are not, and informing the institution of his decision.

§ 4 ° The suspensive act shall also be issued if the period provided for in § 2 has elapsed without any manifestation from the institution.

§ 5 Once the exemption has been suspended:

I - the institution may, within thirty days of being informed, lodge an objection to the declaratory act, which will be decided by the competent Federal Revenue Office;

II - the federal tax inspectorate will issue an infraction notice, if applicable, demanding the tax credit from the date of the occurrence of the fault giving rise to the suspension, the fine referred to in art. 44 of Law No. 9430, of December 27, 1996, and default interest.

§ 6 ° The challenge to the suspension of the exemption will comply with the other rules governing the tax administrative process.

§ 7 Objections and appeals filed by the entity will not have suspensive effect in relation to the declaratory act being contested.

§ 8 If an infraction notice is issued, the challenges against the declaratory act and against the tax credit demand shall be combined in a single proceeding, to be decided simultaneously.

§ 9 ° *The* provisions of the *caput of* this article shall also apply in the event that the educational entity is disconnected from Prouni, as determined by the Ministry of Education, due to non-compliance with the obligations assumed in the term of adhesion.

Art. 6 In the event of disconnection from Prouni at the request of the private educational institution, the exemption from the contributions and tax referred to in art. 1 will be suspended from the date of the disconnection request, covering the entire period of assessment of the tax or contributions.

Art. 7 This Normative Instruction comes into force on the date of its publication.

JORGE ANTONIO DEHER RACHID.

FSC
www.fsc.org
MIX
Papier | Fördert
gute Waldnutzung
FSC® C083411

Kolibri 360 GmbH
Ferdinand-Jühlke-Straße 7
99095 Erfurt, Deutschland
produktsicherheit@kolibri360.de

Druck:
CPI Druckdienstleistungen GmbH
im Auftrag der
Kolibri 360 GmbH
Ferdinand-Jühlke-Str. 7
99095 Erfurt